ESSENTIAL FASHION ILLUSTRATION DETAILS

ESSENTIAL FASHION ILLUSTRATION DETAILS

ROCKPORT PUBLISHERS
GLOUCESTER MASSACHUSETTS

First published in 2007 in the United States of America by
Rockport Publishers, a member of
Quayside Publishing Group
33 Commercial Street
Gloucester, MA 01930-0589
Telephone: (978) 282-9590
Fax: (978) 283-2742
www.rockpub.com

ISBN-13: 978-1-59253-331-2
ISBN-10: 1-59253-331-0

Publisher: Paco Asensio

Editorial coordinator: Catherine Collin

Illustrations: Maite Lafuente

Introduction: Ana G. Cañizares

Art director: Mireia Casanovas Soley

Graphic design and layout: Anabel Naranjo

English translation: Bridget Vranckx

Editorial project:
maomao publications
C/ Tallers 22 bis, 3º 1ª
08001 Barcelona. Spain
Tel.: +34 93 481 57 22
Fax: +34 93 317 42 08
www.maomaopublications.com

Printed in Spain

Contents

Introduction 6

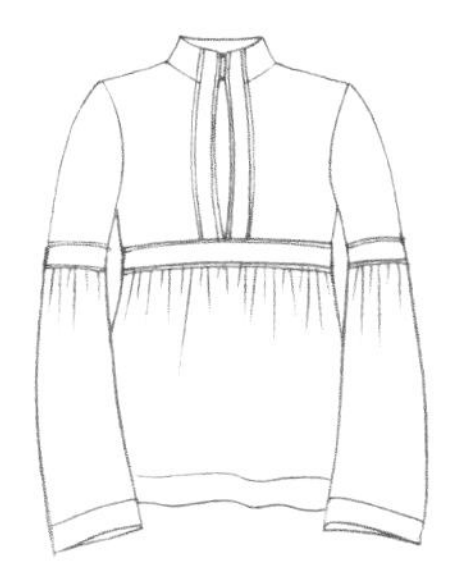

Shirts 8
Tops
Blouses
Vests
& Sweaters

Skirts 52
Dresses
& Pants

Jackets & Coats 104

Lingerie 134
Shoes
& Accessories

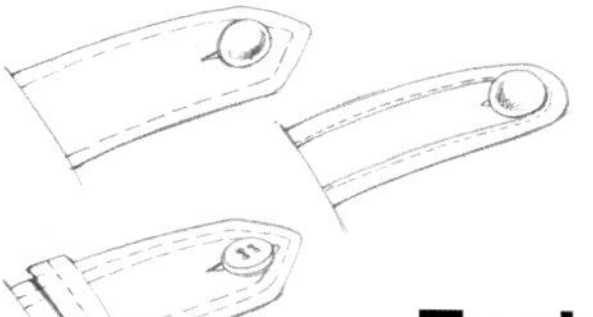

Details 182

Fashion Schools 192
Directory

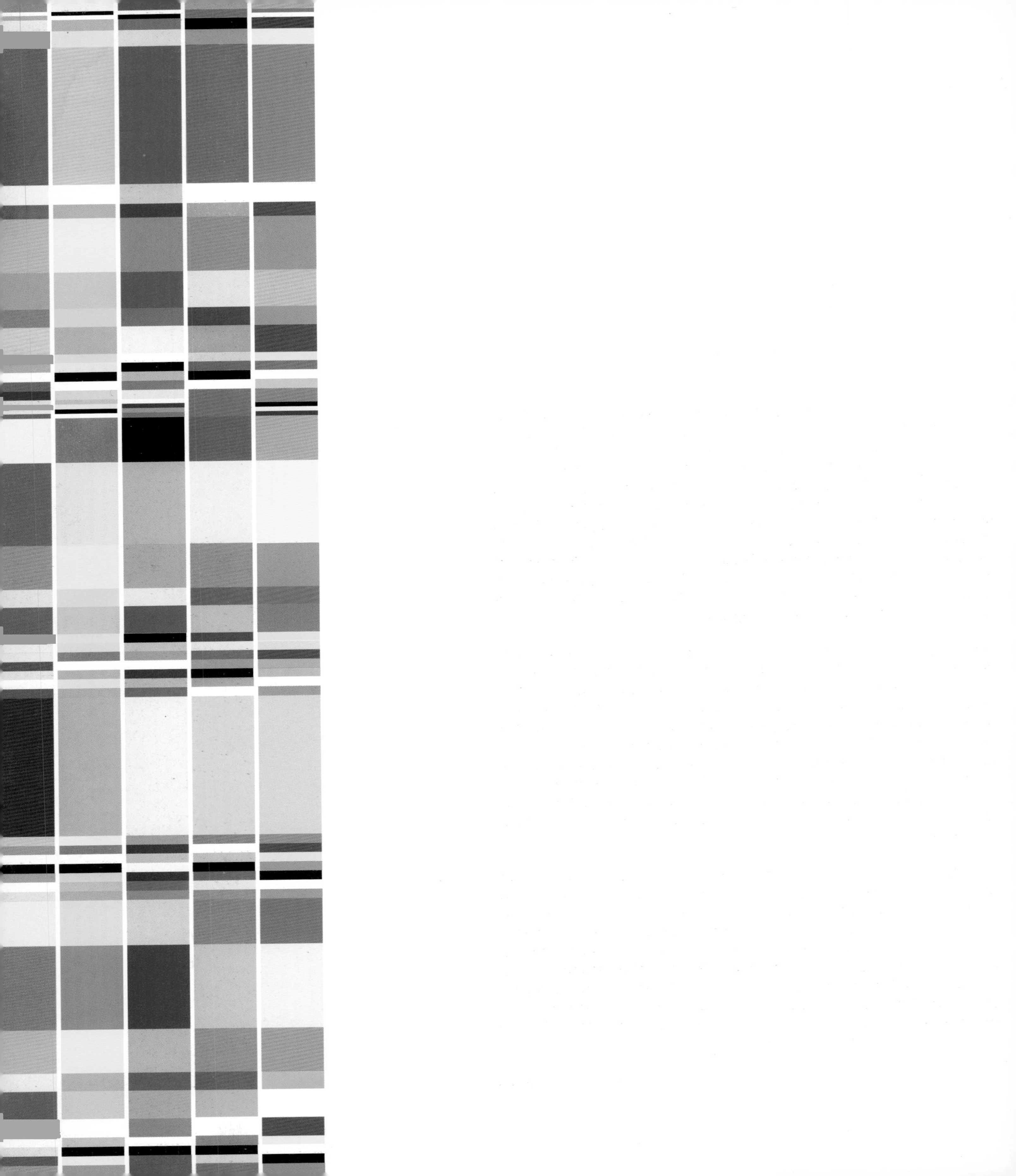

Introduction

Among the many components of fashion illustration, one of the most fundamental is the expression of clothing designs as flat drawings. Despite their apparent simplicity, it is necessary to pay careful attention to certain details that are often overlooked in order to convey the desired shape, volume, and texture of a particular garment. At the same time, the flat drawing proves to be an easier method of illustration than that of drawing three-dimensional human figures, offering the illustrator an equally effective, faster, and less complex way of expressing their ideas. *Essential Fashion Illustration: Details* is perfect for those looking to polish their drawing skills or for those who find difficulty in drawing the human figure and are searching for the right tools to express their clothing designs on paper.

Covering an extensive range of garments including pants, skirts, dresses, shirts, jackets, swimwear, and underwear, this compilation of flat drawings provides a complete overview of the different varieties within each garment and features the styles that have been the most relevant throughout the history of the wardrobe. An essential part of any design, accessories like shoes and hats have also been included to aid designers in achieving the most complete design possible. Most important, however, the illustrations will serve as a reminder to pay attention to crucial details such as stitching, pleats, and wrinkles, which often make all the difference in lending a realistic character to a drawing.

Flat drawings, although perhaps less visually attractive in comparison to other techniques, form an indispensable part of fashion illustration. A basic and straightforward representation of a garment as a flat drawing is the first step in expressing an idea for a design on paper, and given their simplicity, must be executed with perfection in order to convey all of the qualities and characteristics of a particular piece. *Essential Fashion Illustration: Details* intends to provide those looking to develop their own drawing skills with a practical and useful source of inspiration that holds the keys to mastering the art of the flat drawing in the world of fashion design.

Ana G. Cañizares

Shirts
Tops
Blouses
Vests
& Sweaters

Shirts

Shirt with smock stitch down middle

Draped neckline. Asymmetric drop. Wide-flared sleeves.

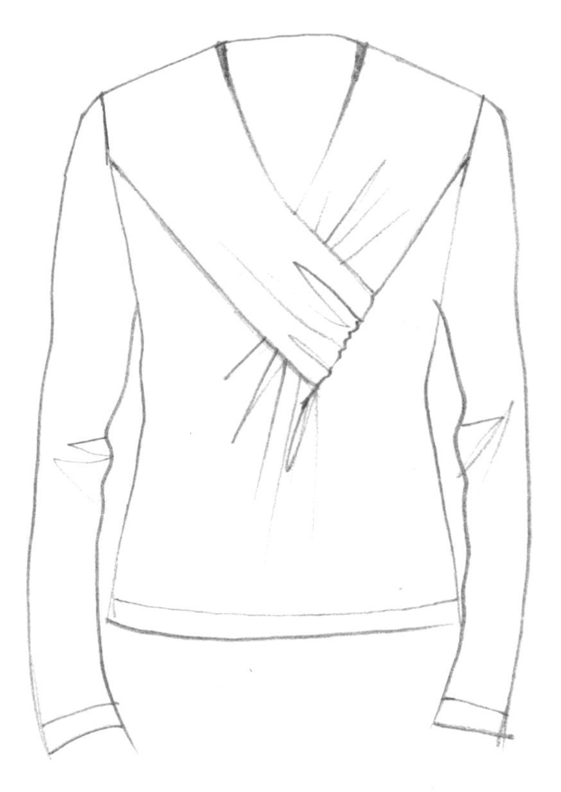

Shirt with draped traverse

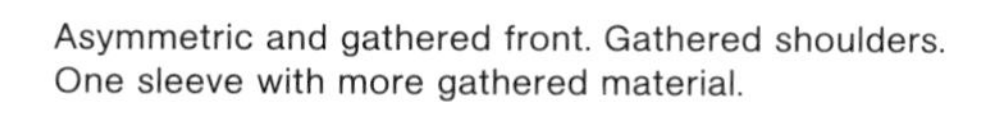

Asymmetric and gathered front. Gathered shoulders.
One sleeve with more gathered material.

Two pieces of fabric: one fin, long and gathered below the bust. The other compact. Button and loop closure.

Shank neck, 3/4-length sleeves, button and loop fasteners and gatherings at the shoulders.

Draped front crossing

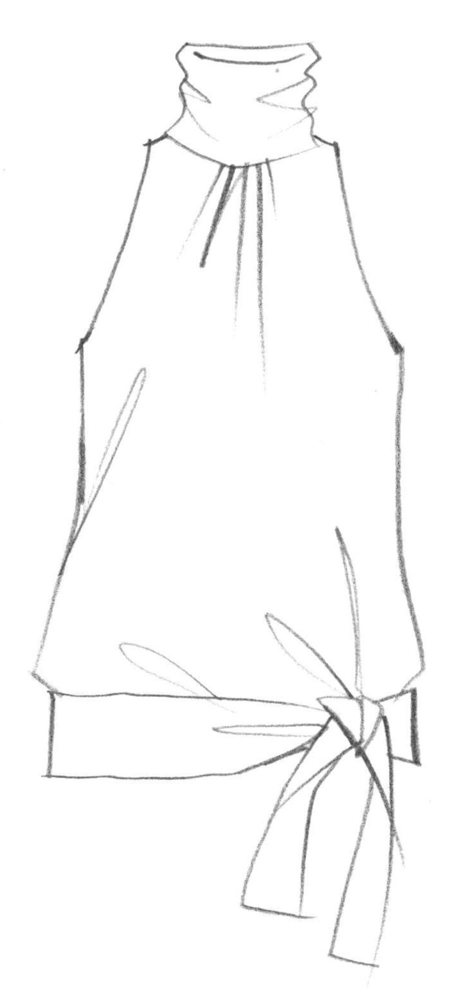

Gathered turtleneck. Low knotted waist. American armhole.

Tunic tucked at the hip and gatherings below the bust

Ballooned with double fabric and gathered.
Crossed straps on the back.

Mini-dress with two pieces of fabric: one finer superimposed and more compact at the bottom.

Ballooned. Gathered yoke.

Scoop neck. Fitted at the sides and 3/4-length convex sleeves. Elastic cuffs.

Gathered with elastic in the center of the garment

Tops

Flared tops with trimming

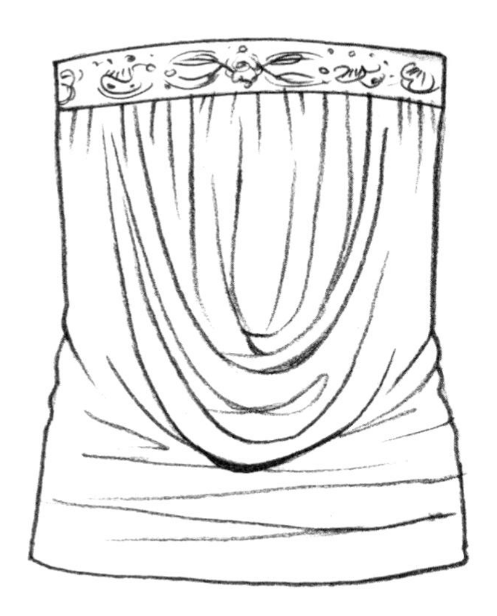

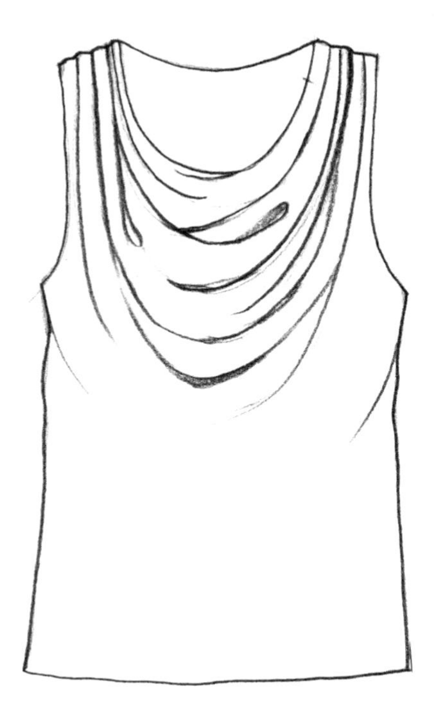

Draped tops

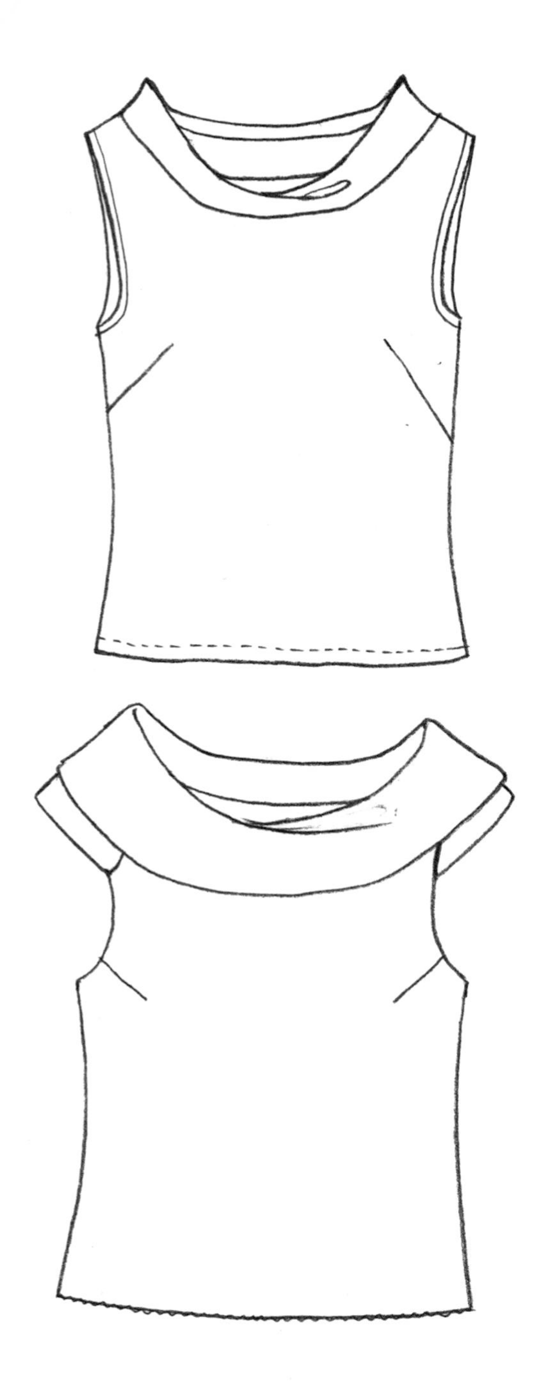

Tops with stretched collar

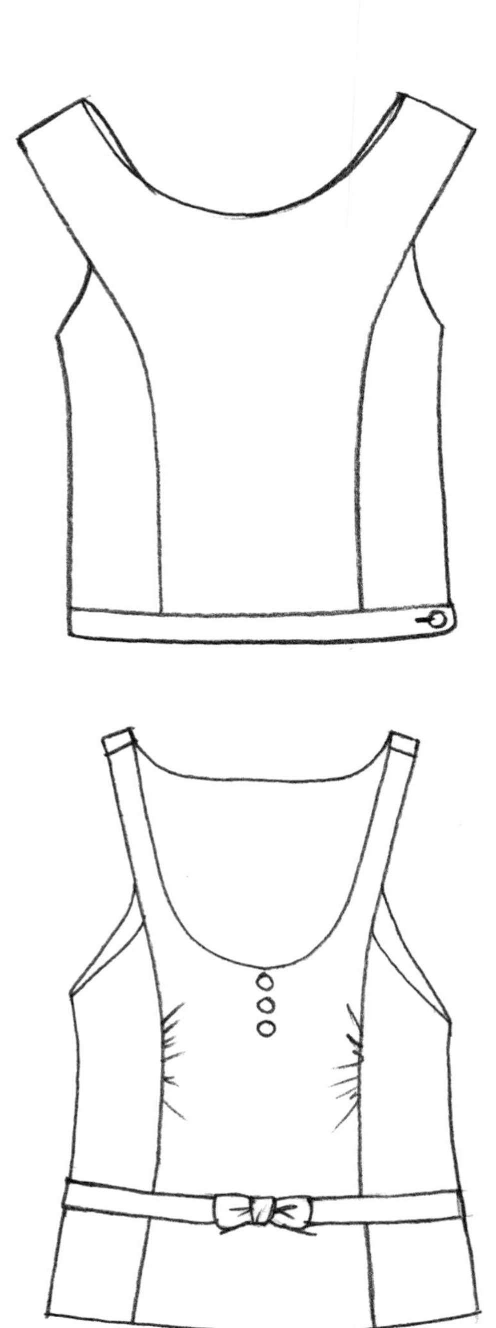

Retro tops with belt

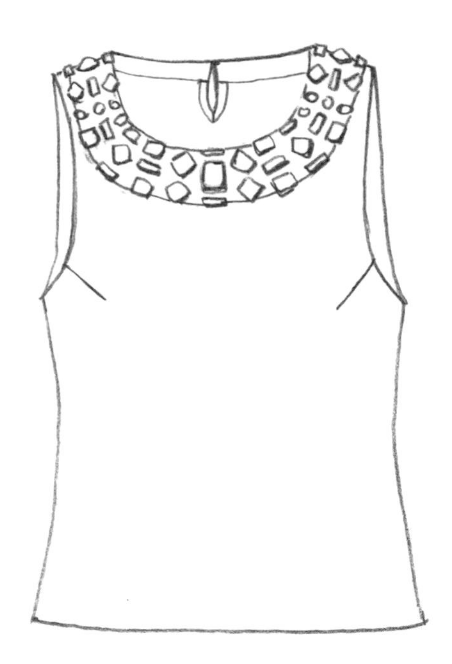

Bustier

Beaded tops

Bathing-style top

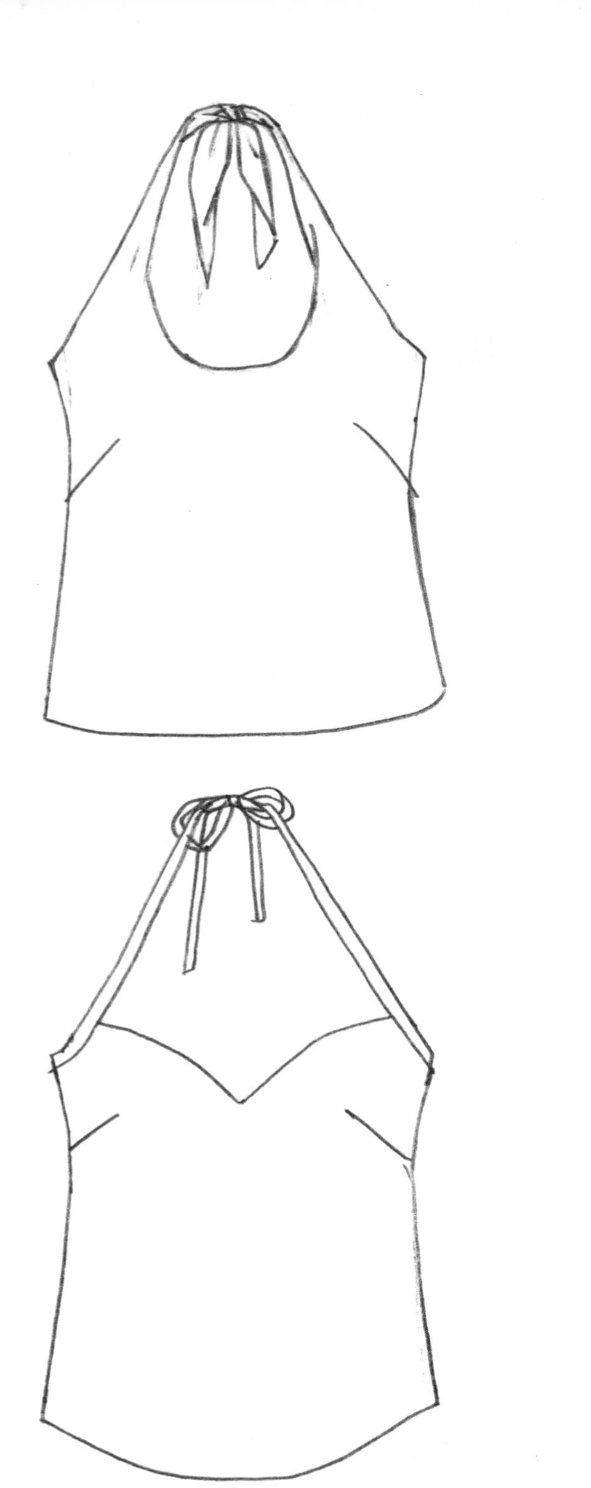

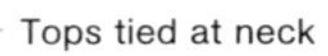

Tops tied at neck

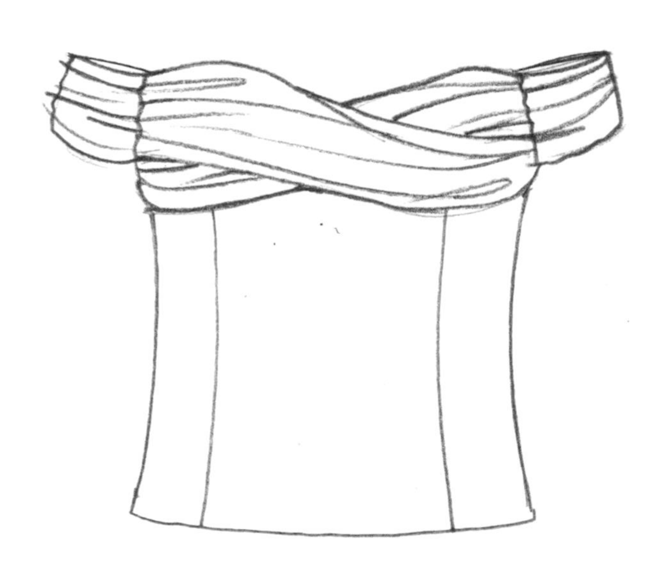

Draped tops

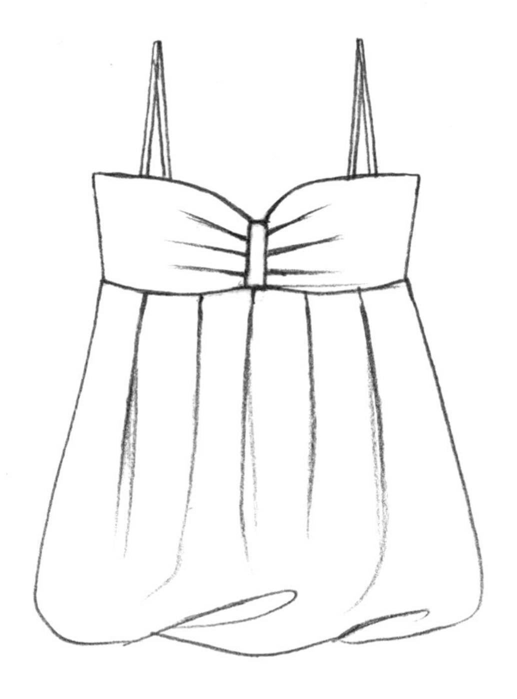

Balloon top with straps

Empire-style tops

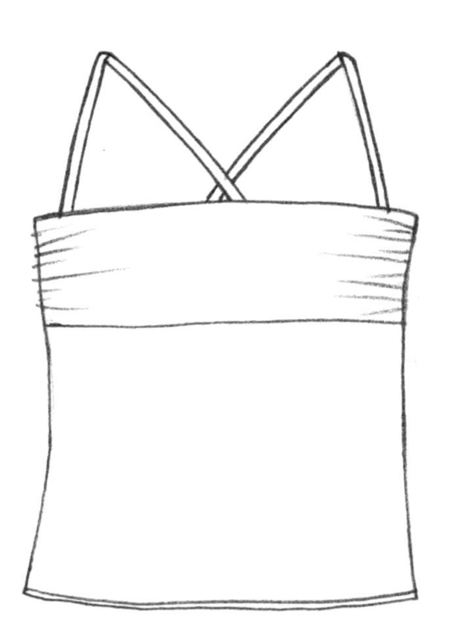

Top with crossed straps

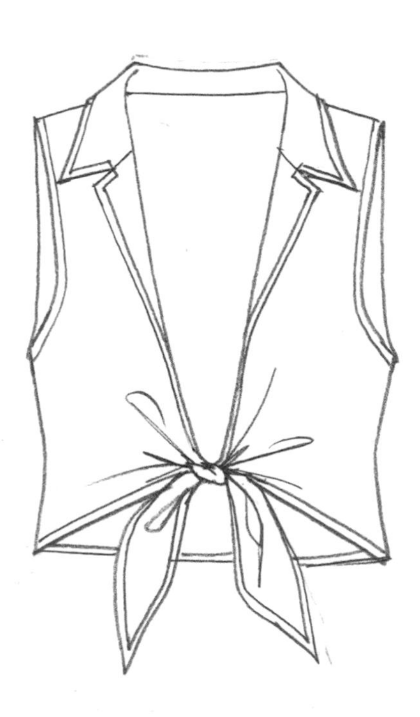

Knotted sleeveless top

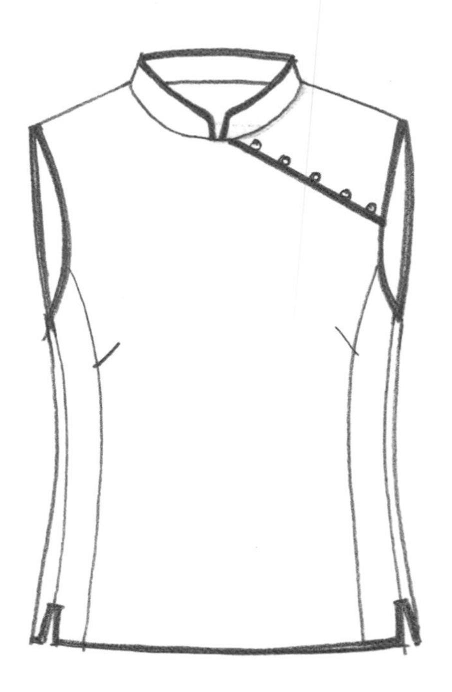

Chinese-buttoned top

Crew neck top

Top with stretched collar

Blouses

Caftan blouse

"Biarritz" blouse

Tie-neck blouse

Blouse with tied collar

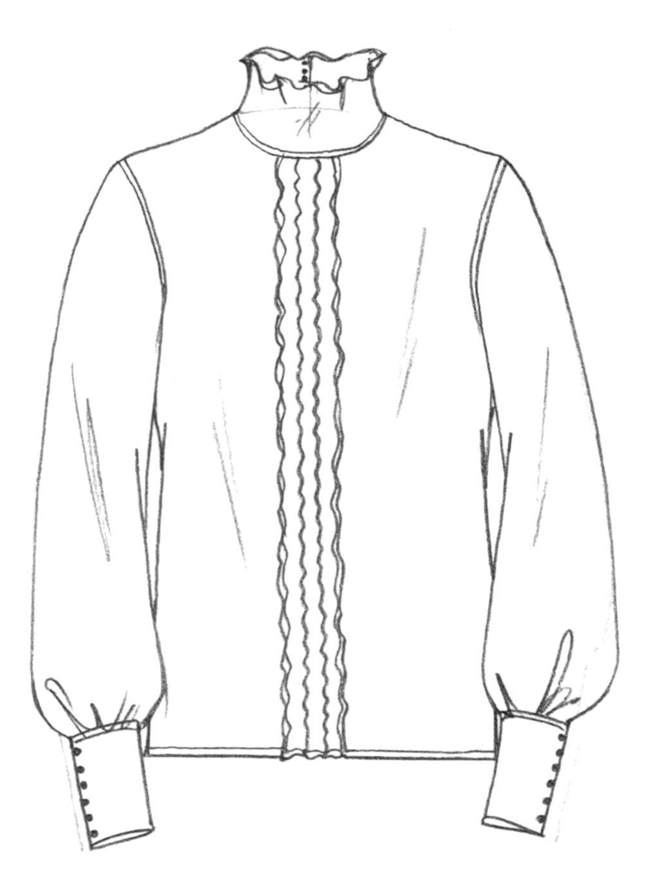
Blouse with Victorian collar

Lace blouse with shirt front

Smock

Blouse with ruff

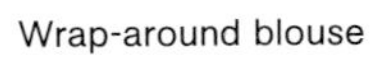
Wrap-around blouse

"Zingara" blouse

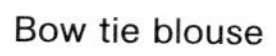

Bow tie blouse

Classic blouse

Denim shirt, *front*

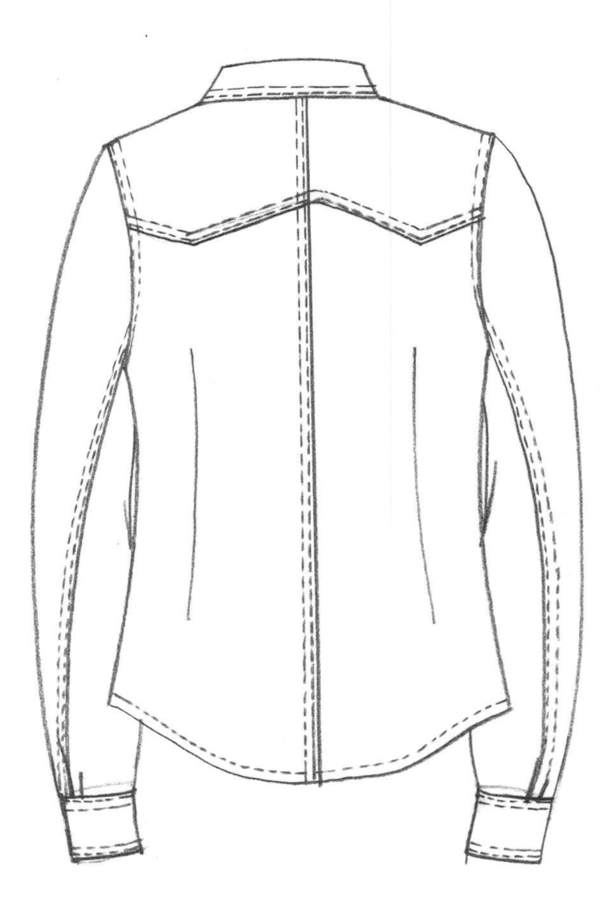

Denim shirt, *back*

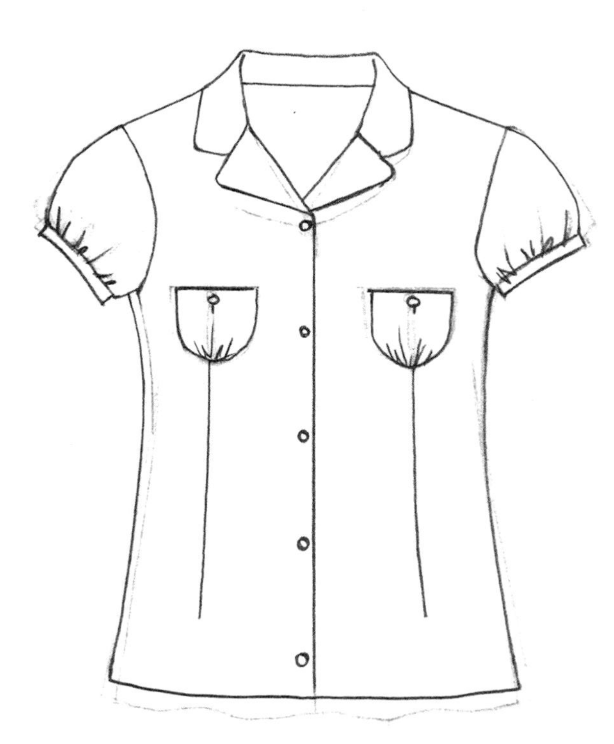

Retro blouse

Round-collared blouse with gathered sleeves

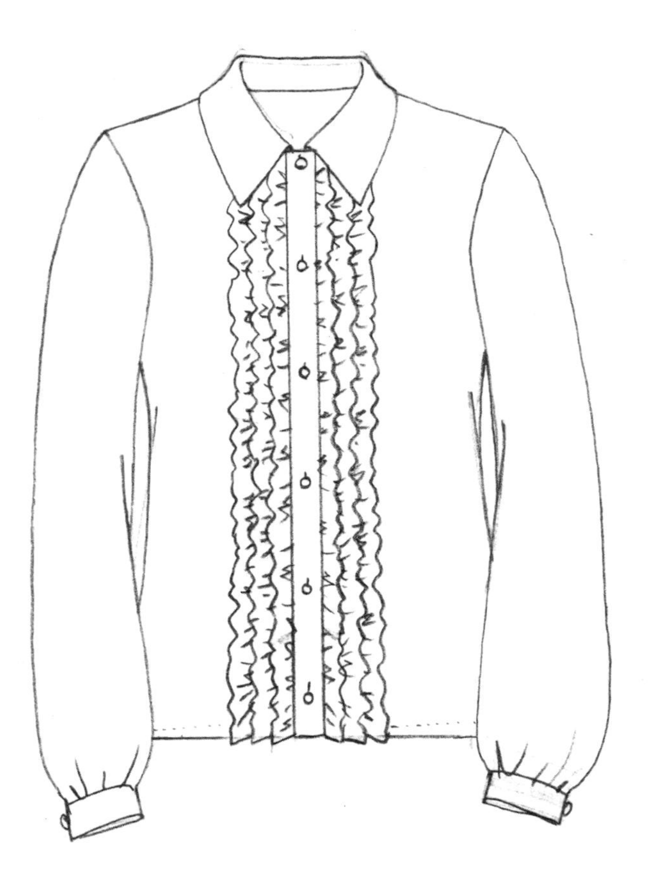

Ruffle-fronted blouse

Buttoned blouse with pleated breast

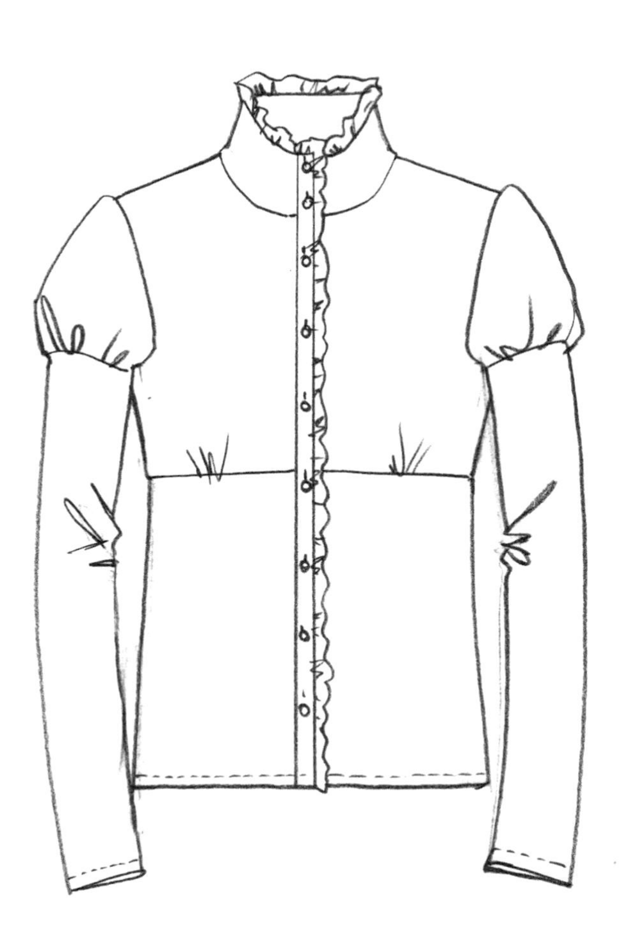

Victorian blouse

“Peasant” blouse

Vests

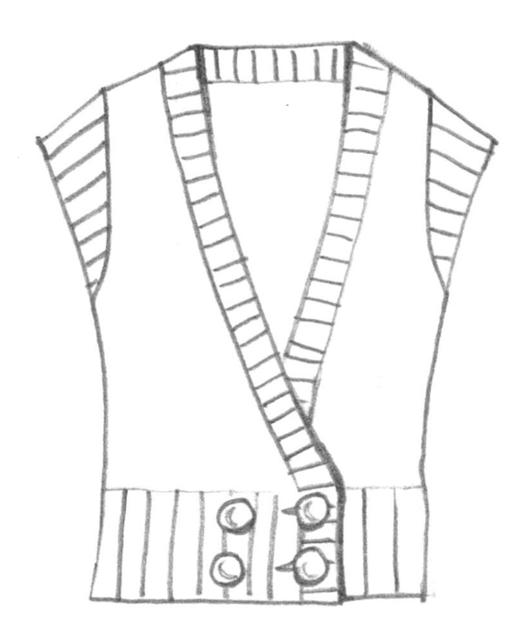

Thick double-breasted

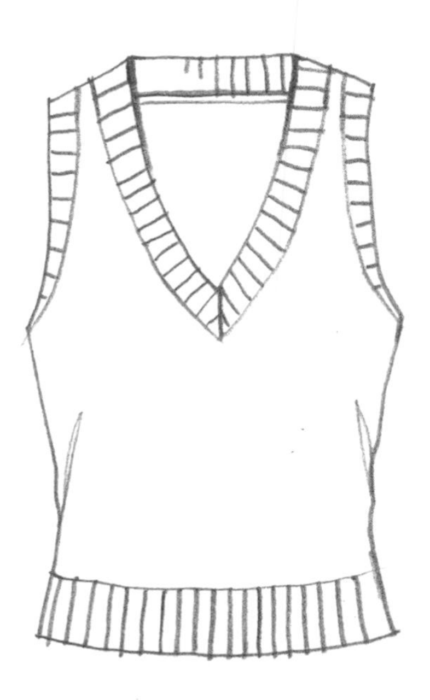

Closed with wide ribbing

Closed and tight

Low-necked

Sweaters

Low-necked with 3/4-length sleeves

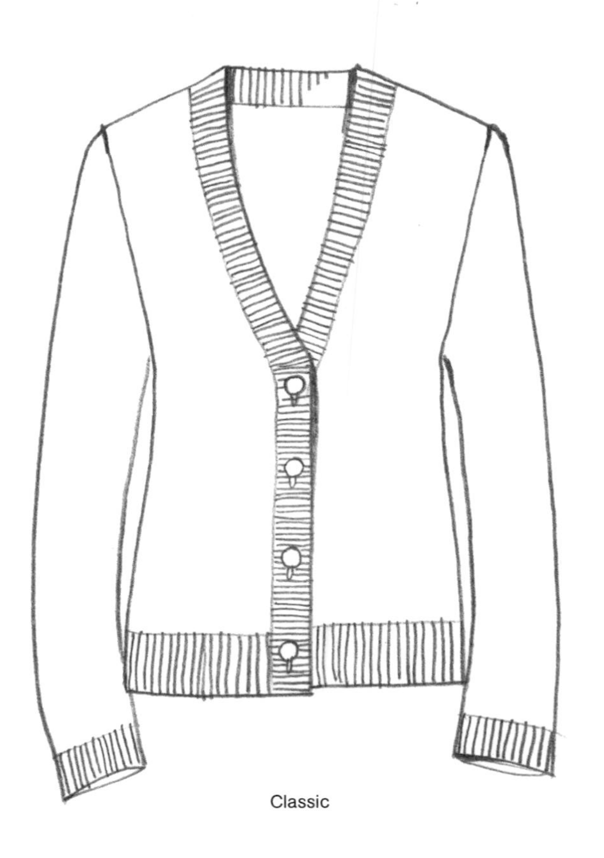

Classic

Classic cardigan

Twin set

Double-breasted

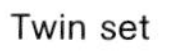

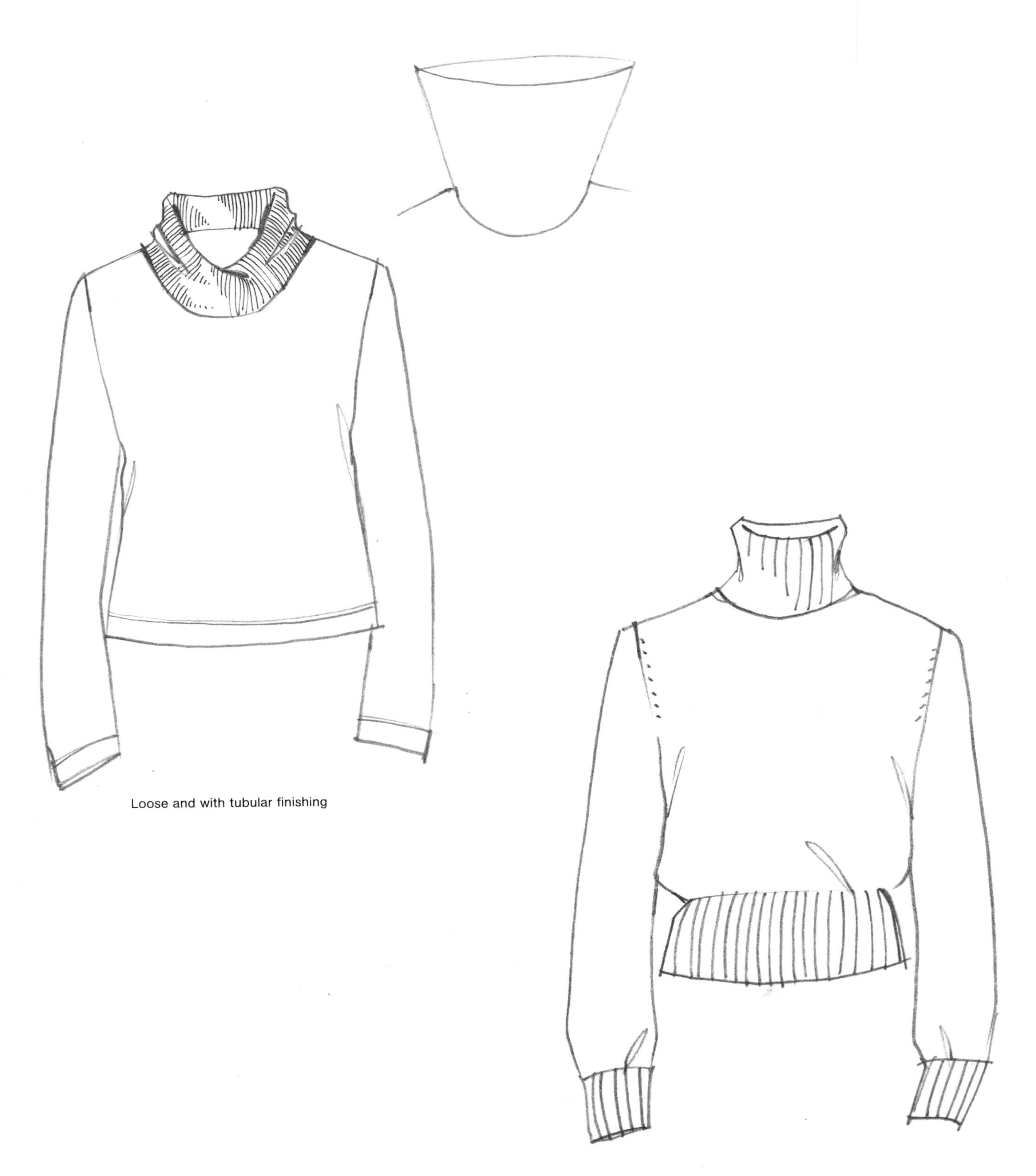

Loose and with tubular finishing

Classic thick turtleneck with wide ribbing on bottom and cuffs.

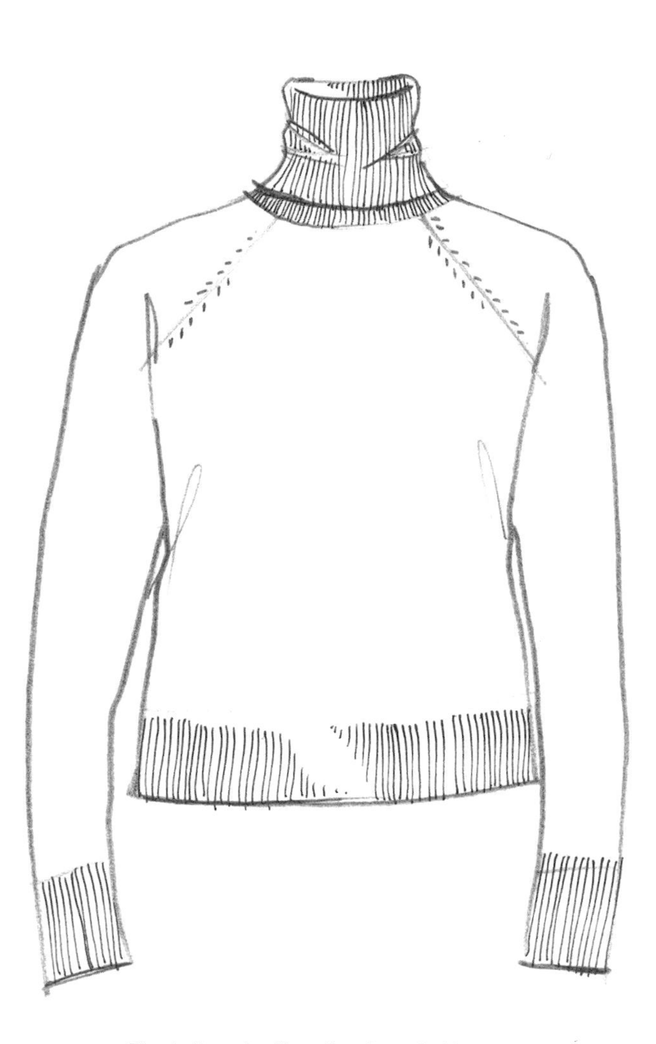

Fine turtleneck with raglan sleeve fashioning. Wide ribbing on bottom and cuffs.

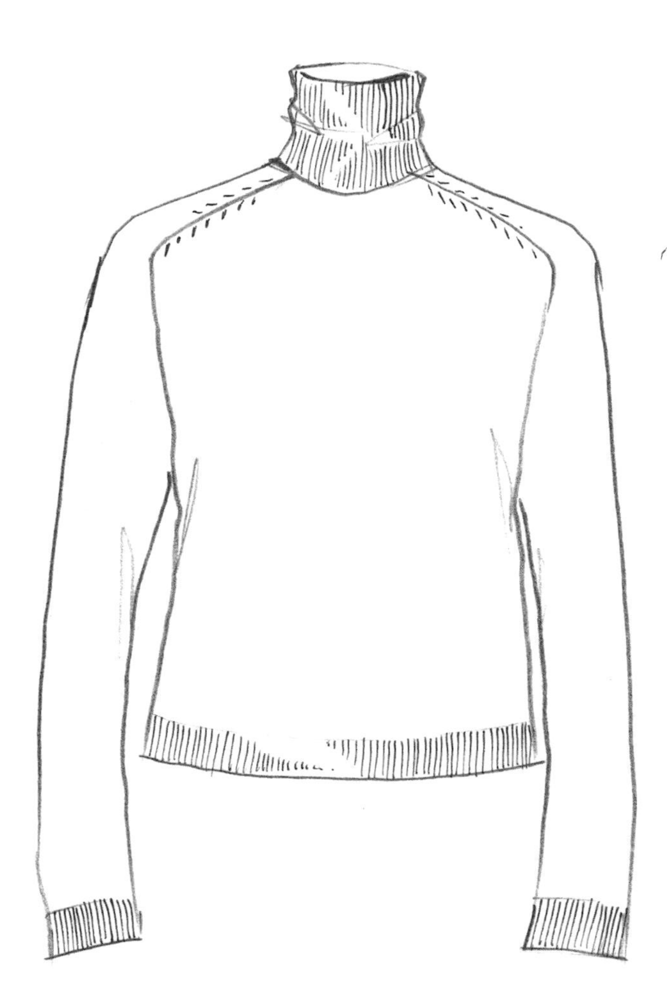

Fine turtleneck with hammer sleeve fashioning

Ribbed turtleneck

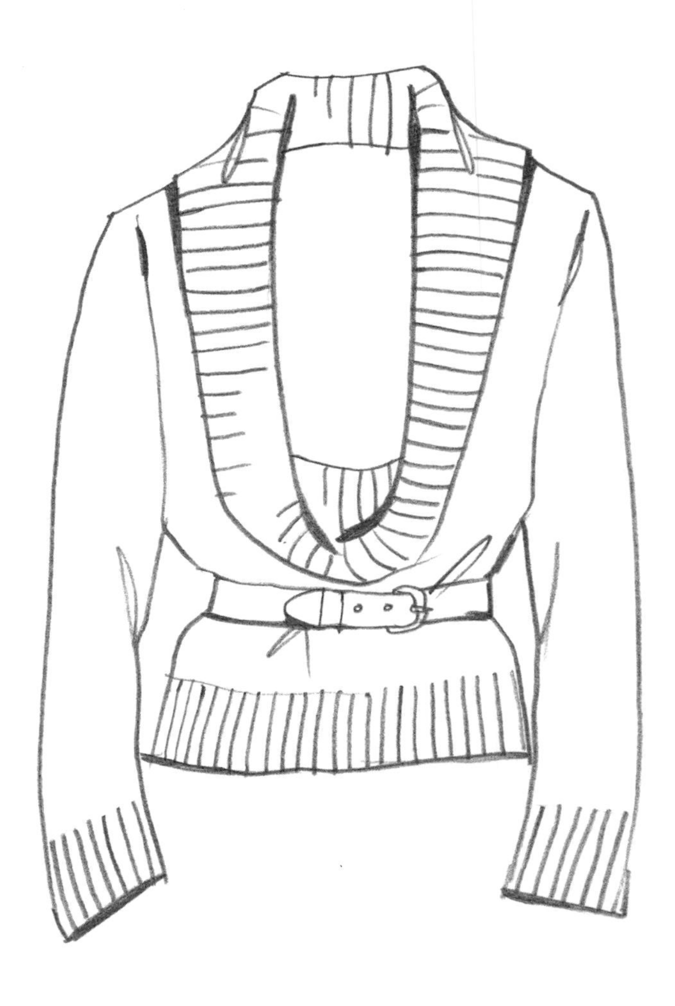

Thick turtleneck, loose and low neckline.

Short dress with thick and loose turtleneck

Thick turtleneck with 3/4-length Japanese sleeves

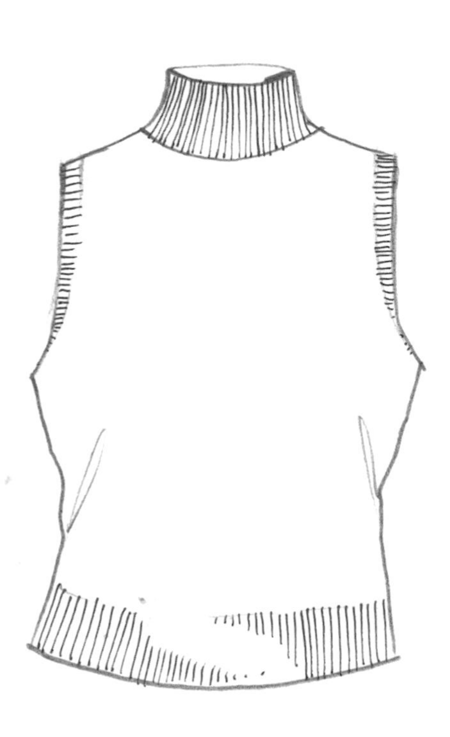

Semifine turtleneck. Sleeveless.

Fine turtleneck with middle parting. Bottom and cuffs very wide. Loose fitting line.

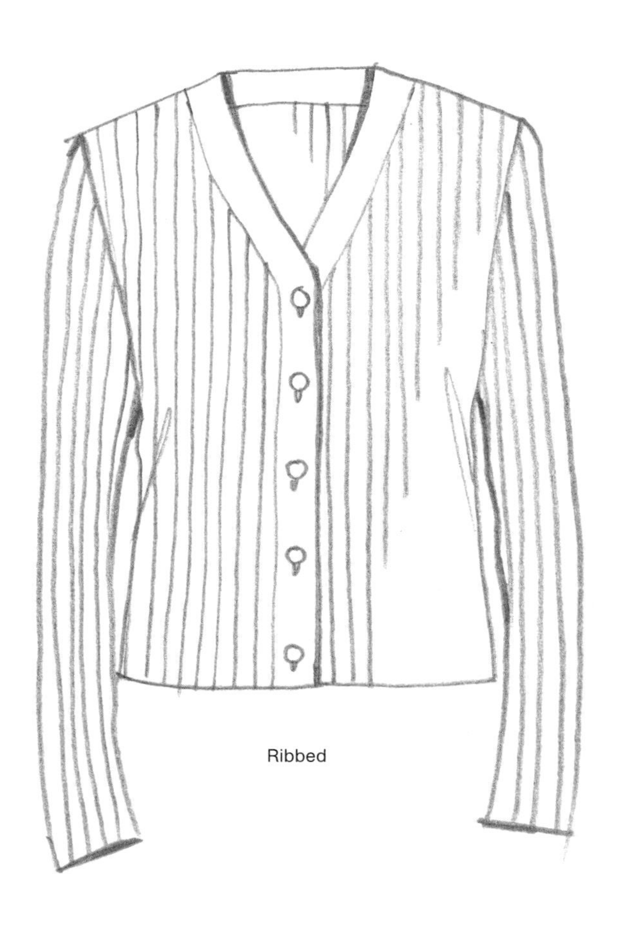

Ribbed

With belt, pushed up sleeves and flat strip

With bow and flat strip

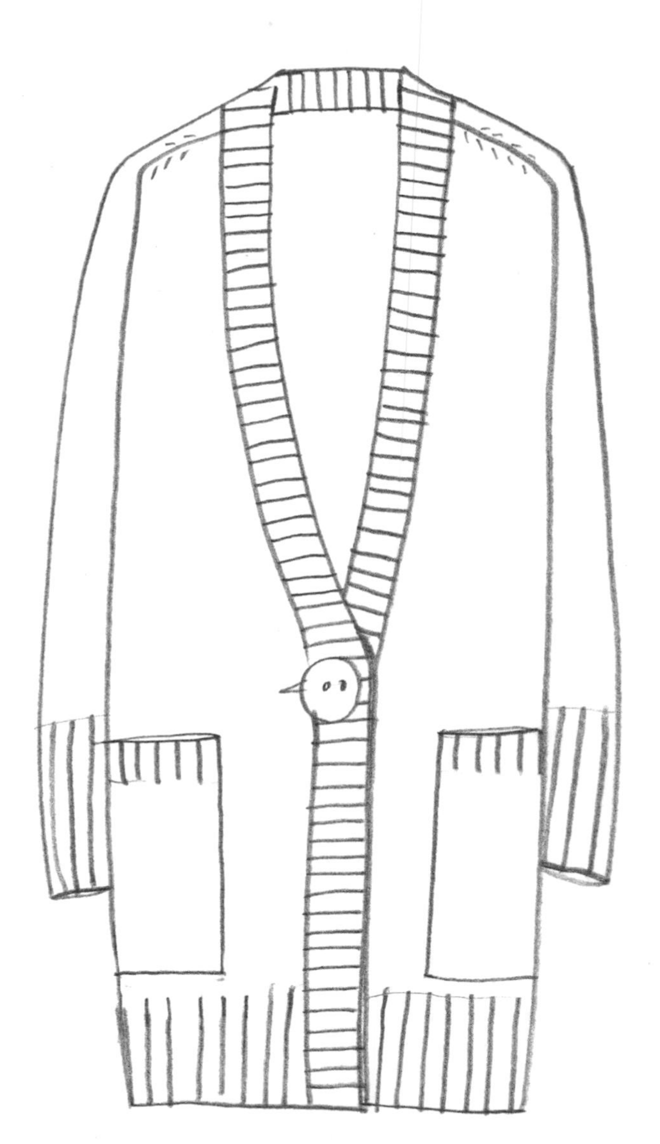
3/4 length and thick

With shirt neckline

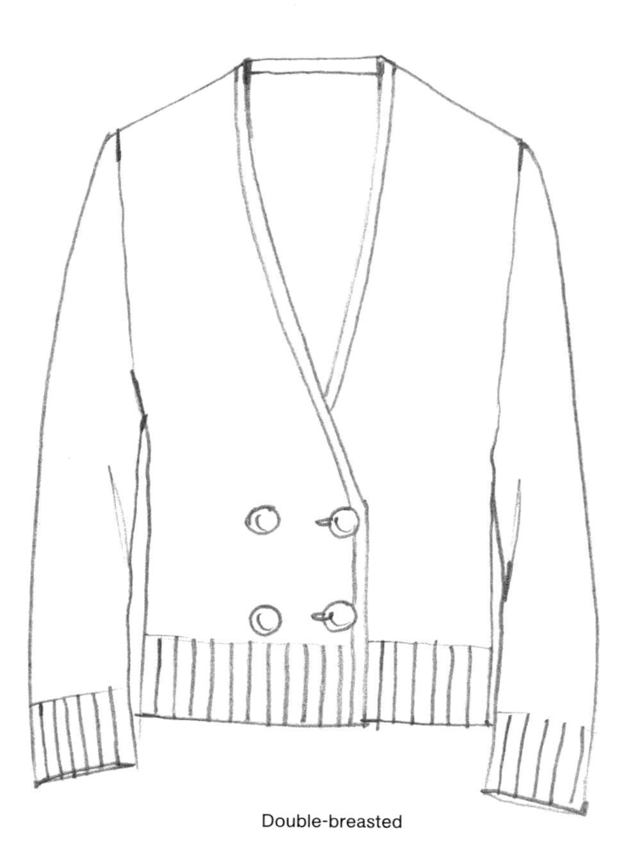

Double-breasted

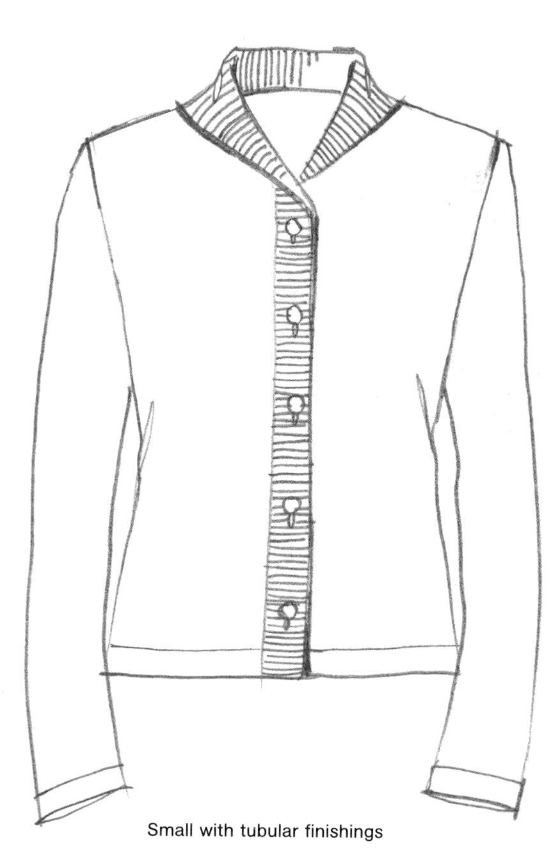

Small with tubular finishings

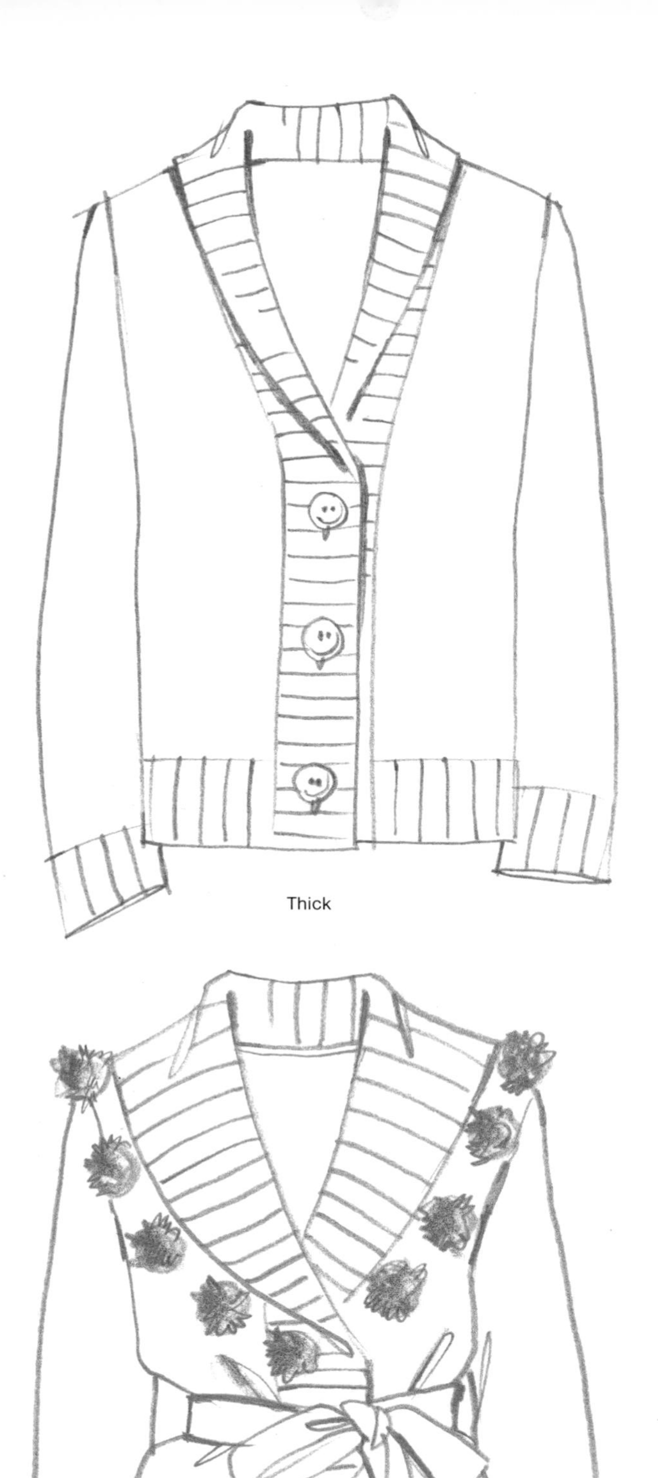

Thick

Fancy smoking cardigan with
pom-poms and satin bow belt.

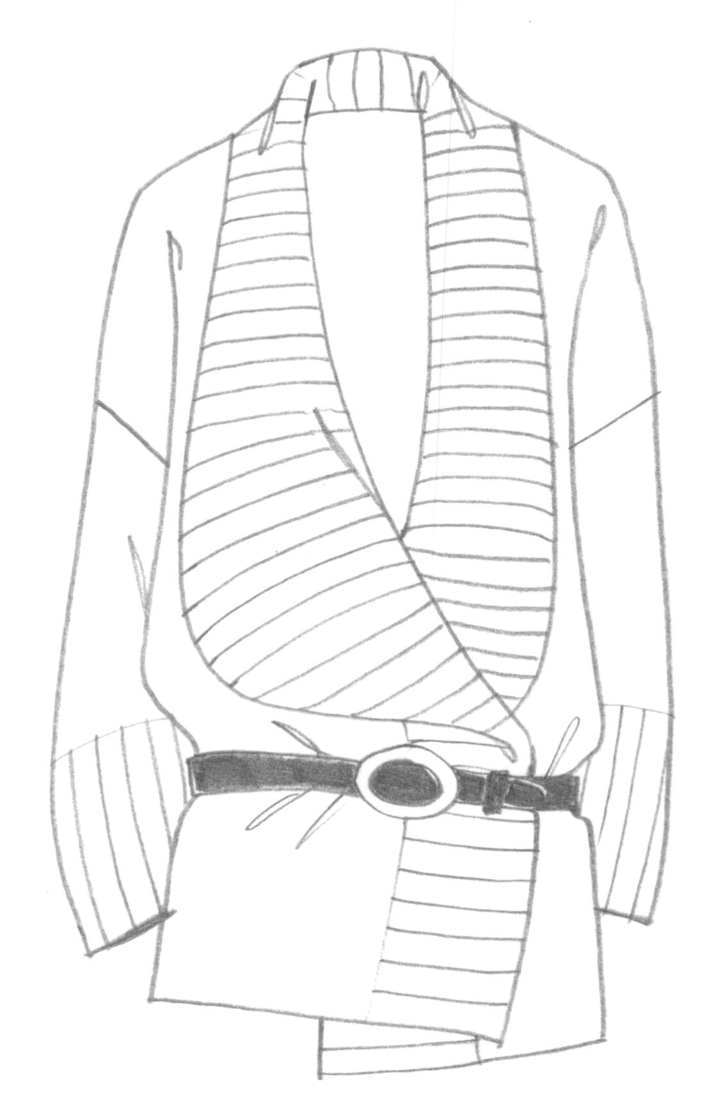

Very exaggerated finishings and unstructured thick cut

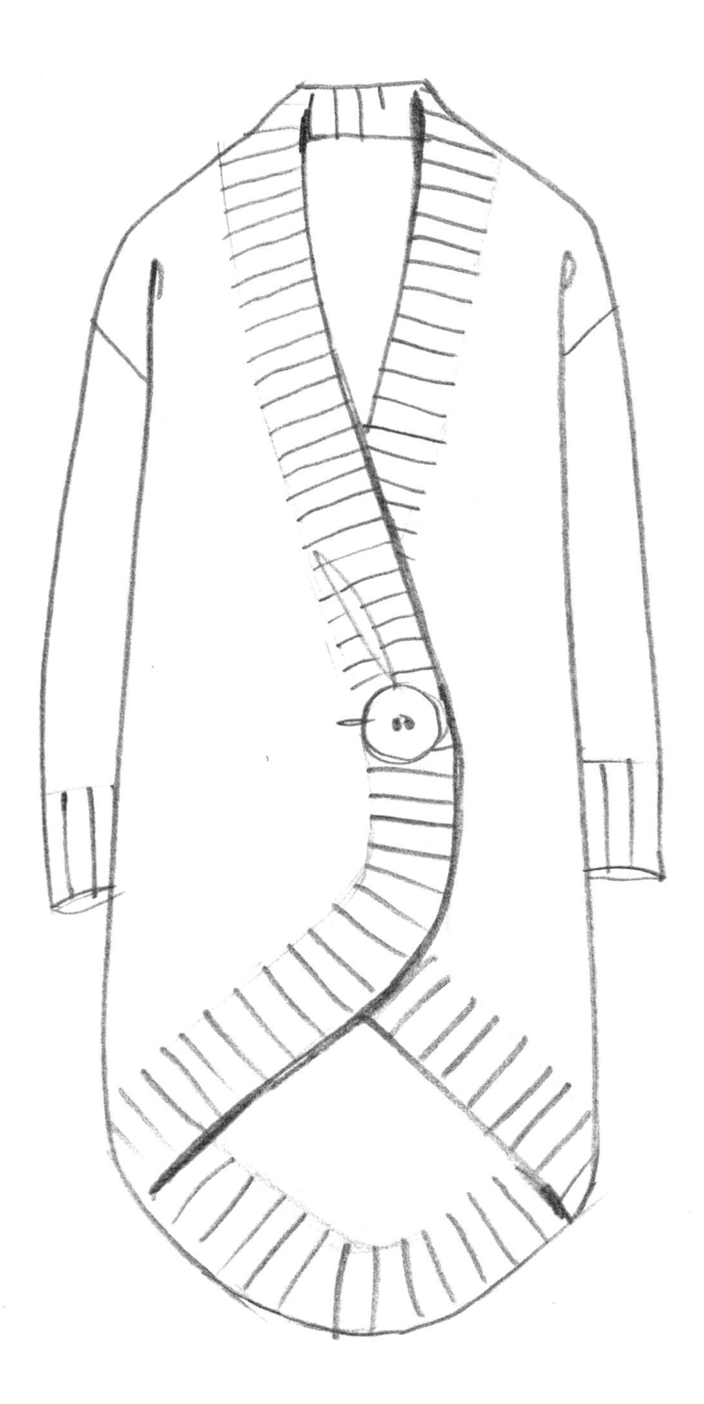
Asymmetric coat

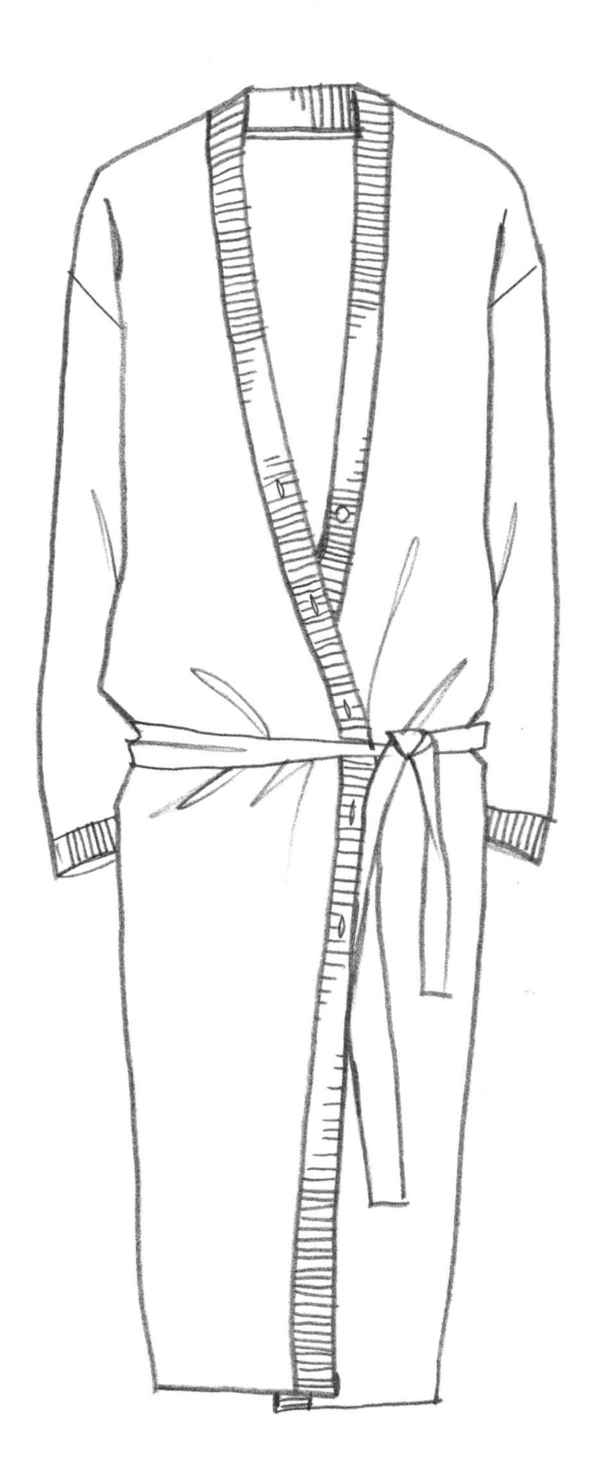
Long and tied at the hip

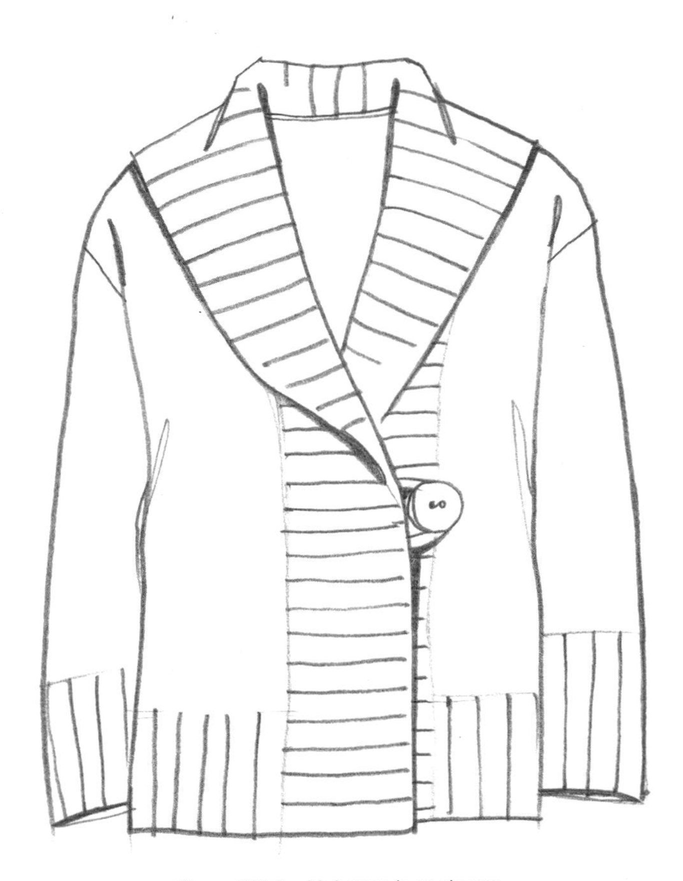

Big and thick with button-loop closure

With high neck

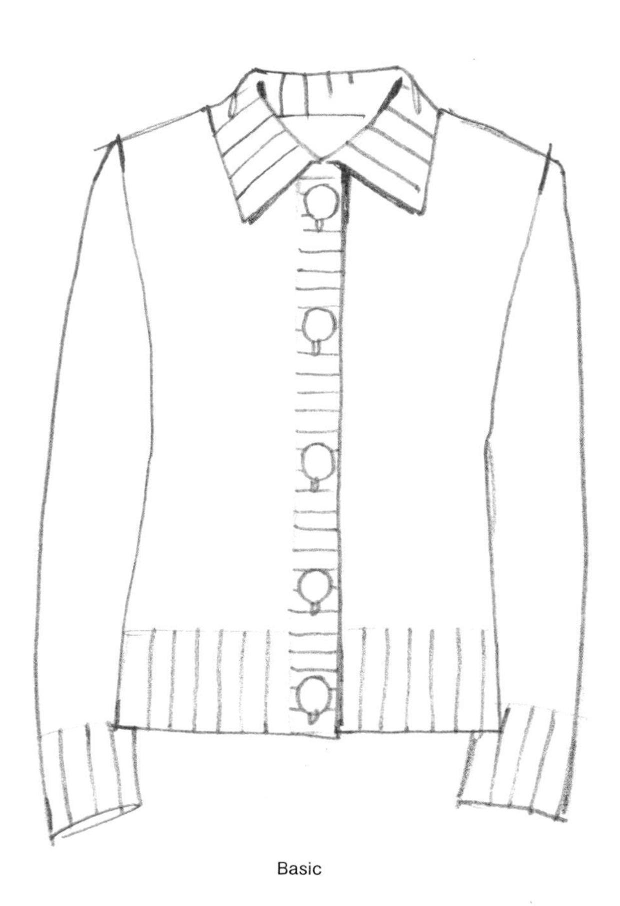
Basic

With shank collar

With fur collar

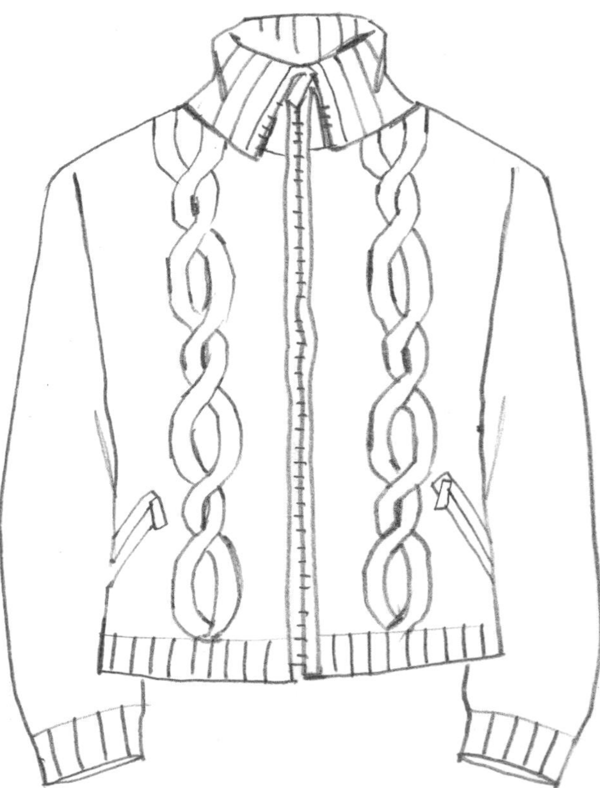

With turtleneck and braids

Shirt collar

Shawl/Bolero

Very light, knotted and with overlock finishings

Skirts Dresses & Pants

Skirts

Pleated skirt

Scottish kilt

Split skirt

A-line skirt

Tulip skirt

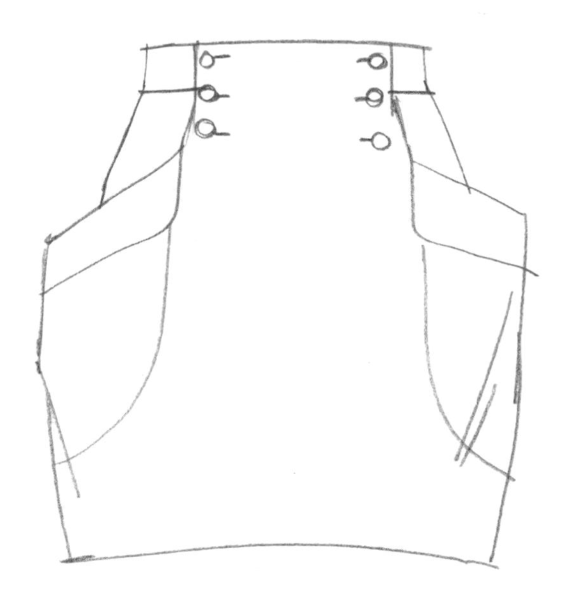

Sack skirt

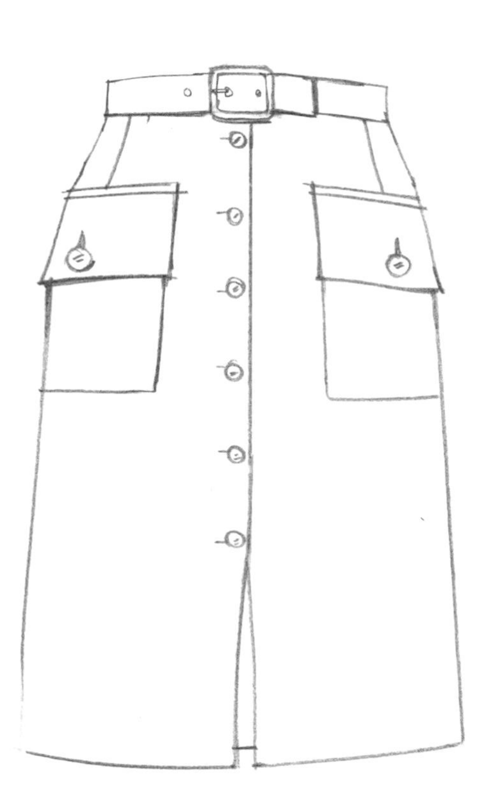

Military-style skirt

Poof skirt

Ballerina skirt

Ruffle skirt

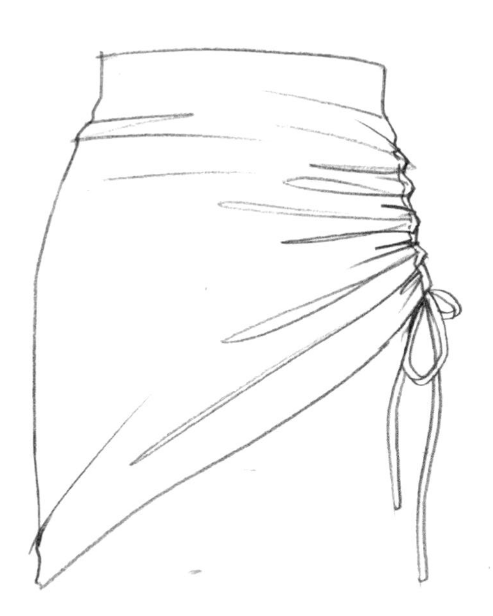
Straight skirt with side tuck

Balloon skirt

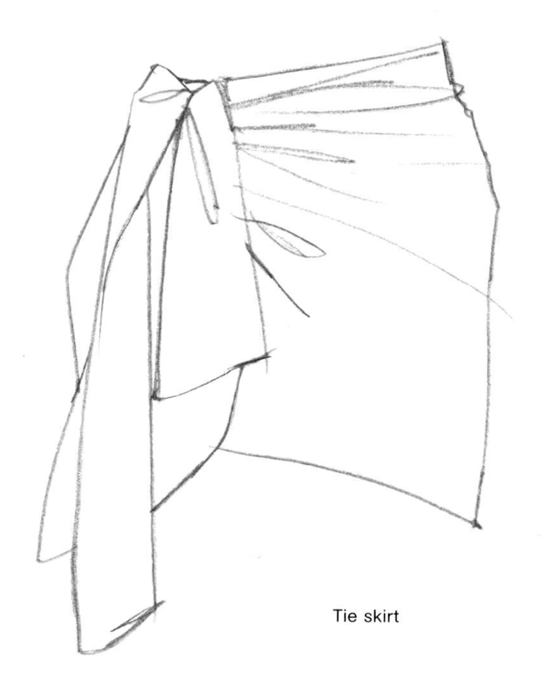

Tie skirt

Cocktail skirt with ruffles and netting

"Boulonne" skirt

Skirt with side slits

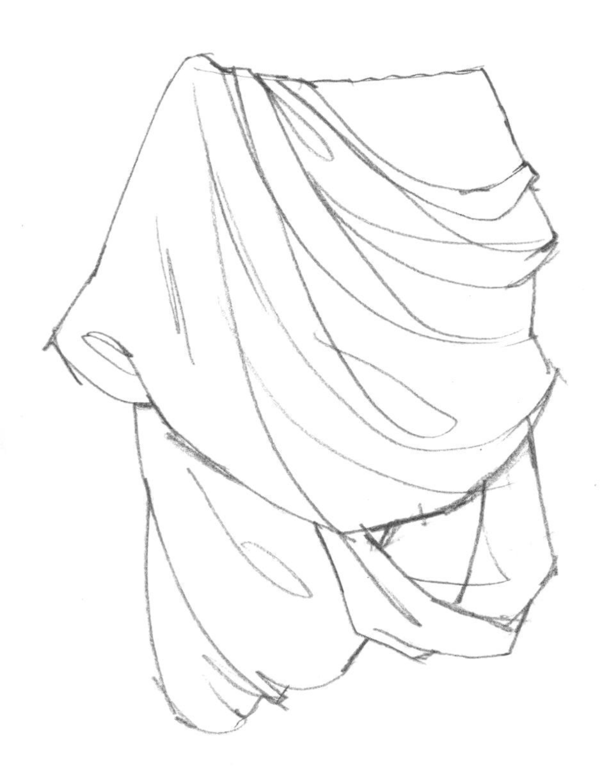

“Godess” or toga skirt

Draped skirt

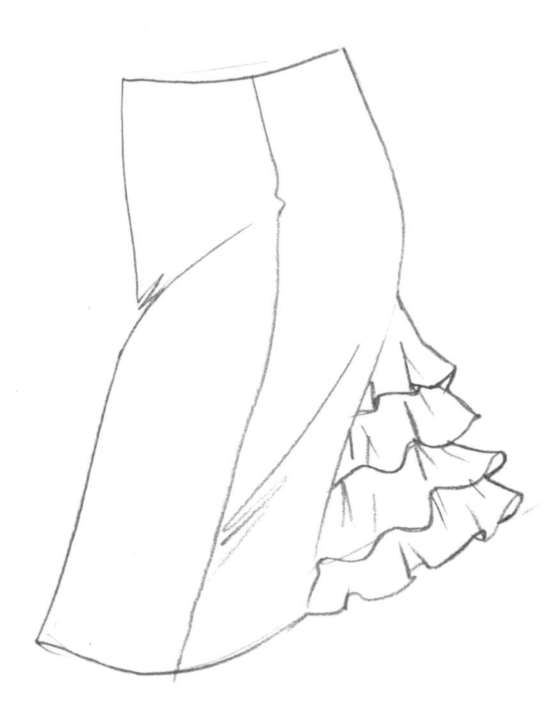

Profile view of skirt with ruffles on back

Creased cocktail skirt

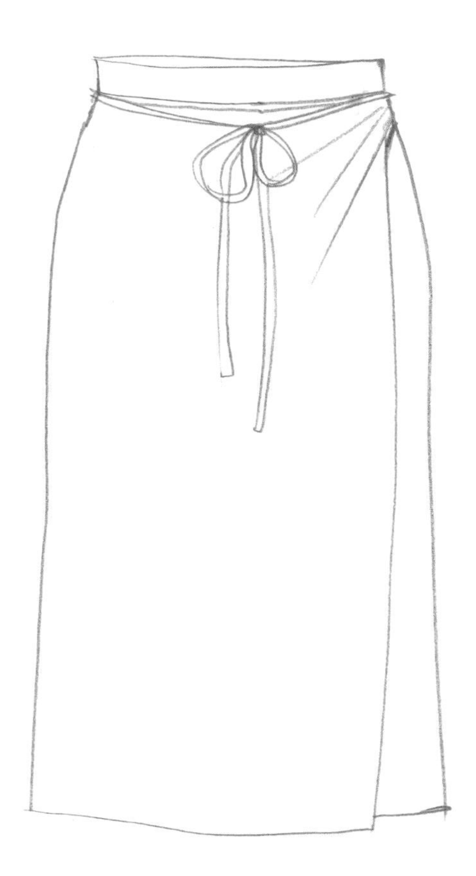

Apron skirt

Skirt with ruffles on the bias

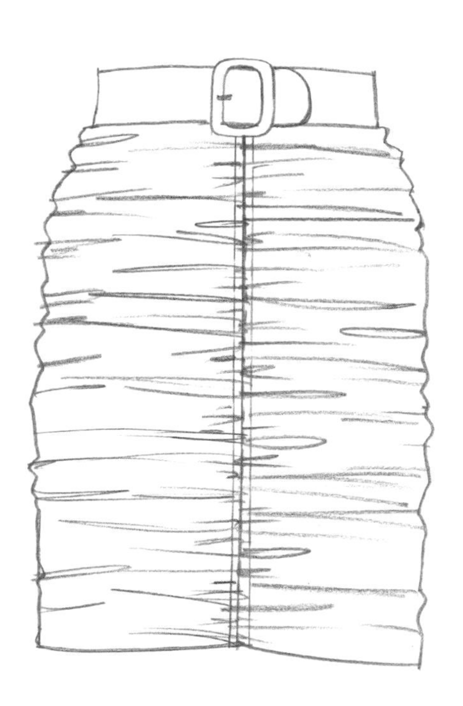

Creased skirt

"Peasant" skirt

Skirt with satin ruffles

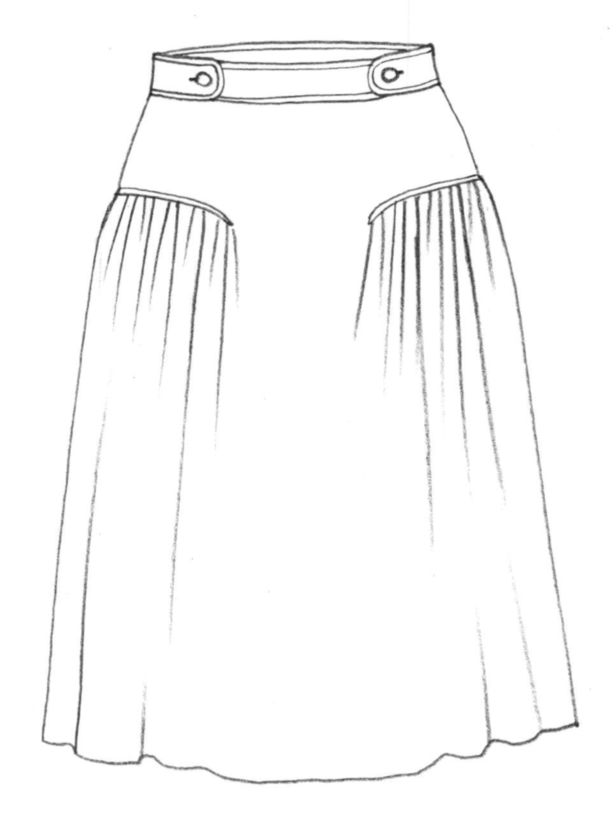

Corolla skirt with welt seams

Skirt with gathering

Tulip skirt

Full skirt with gathering

Skirt with sewn pleats from the hip down

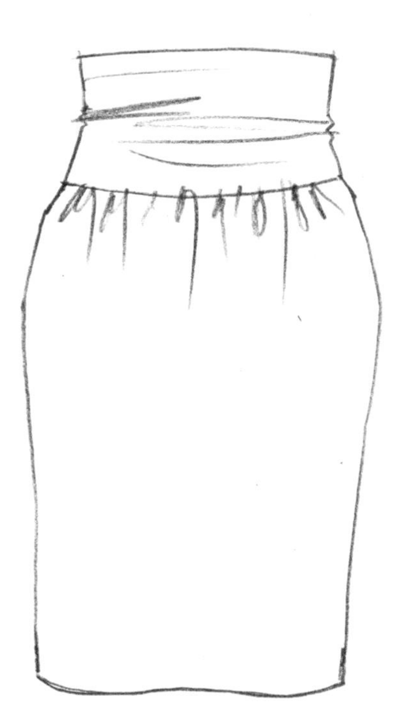

Straight skirt

Sarong

Straight skirt

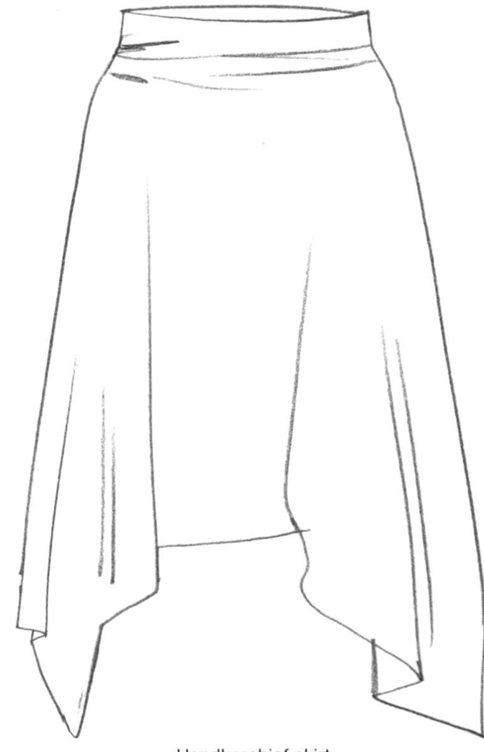

Handkerchief skirt

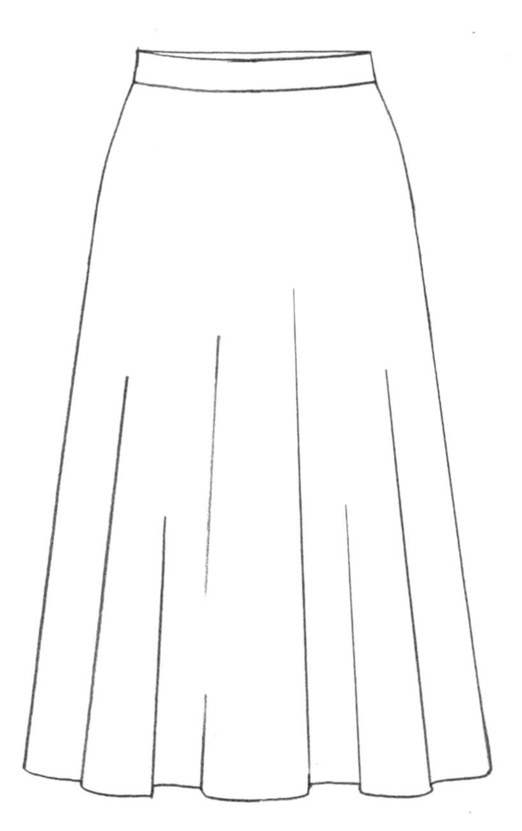

Layered skirt

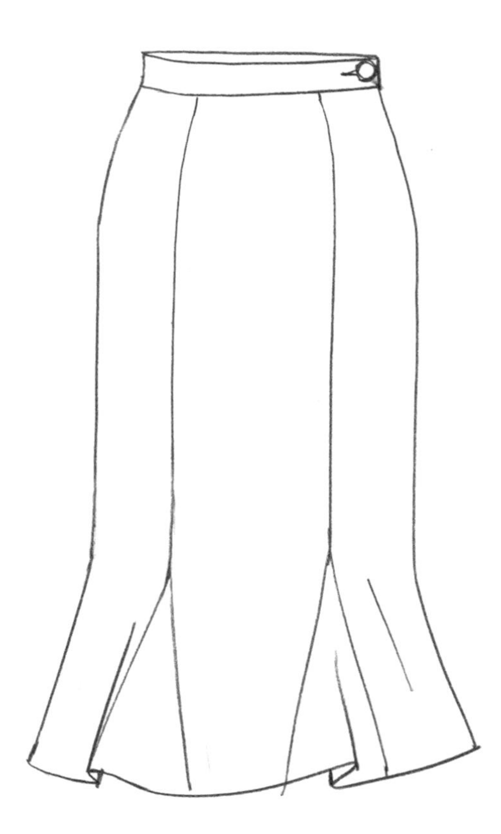

Godet skirt

Can-can skirt with tutu

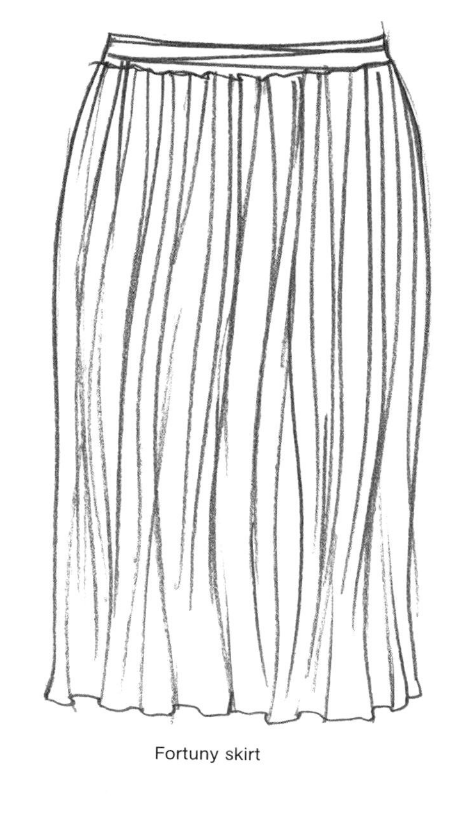
Fortuny skirt

Denim skirt

Safari-style skirt

Dresses

Wrap dress

Empire lace

Polo-shirt dress

Beach dress

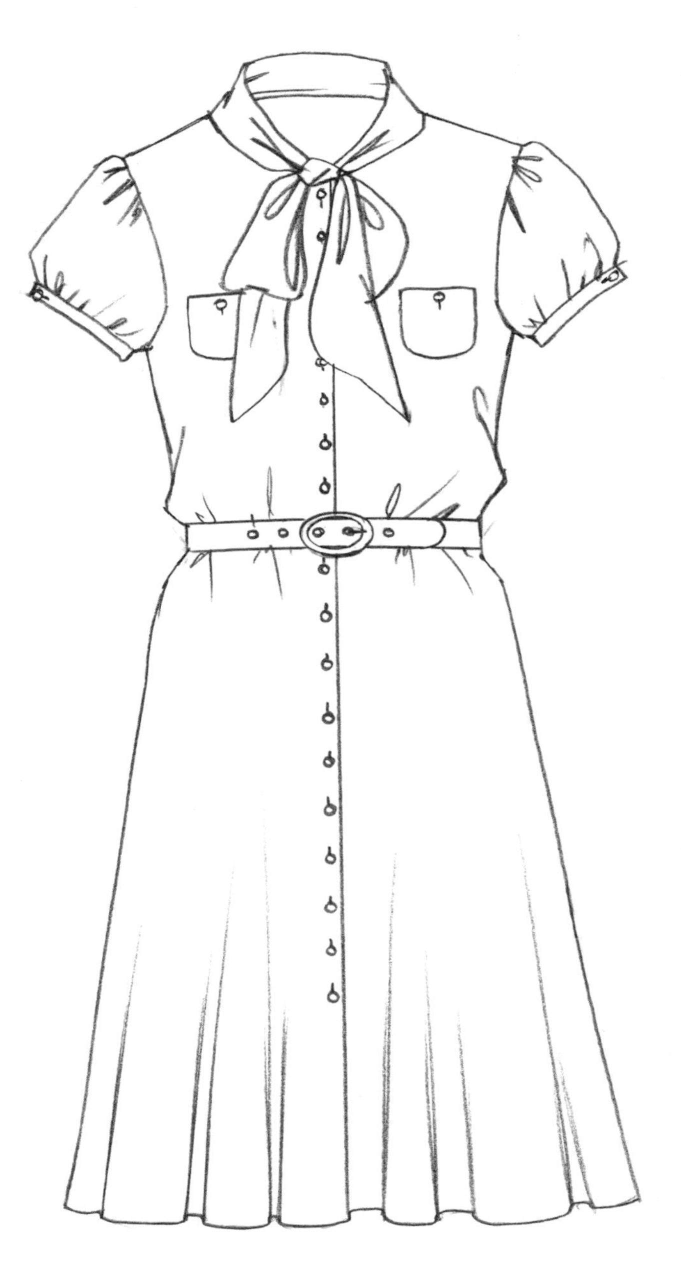

Retro-blouse dress

Dress coat

Shirtdress

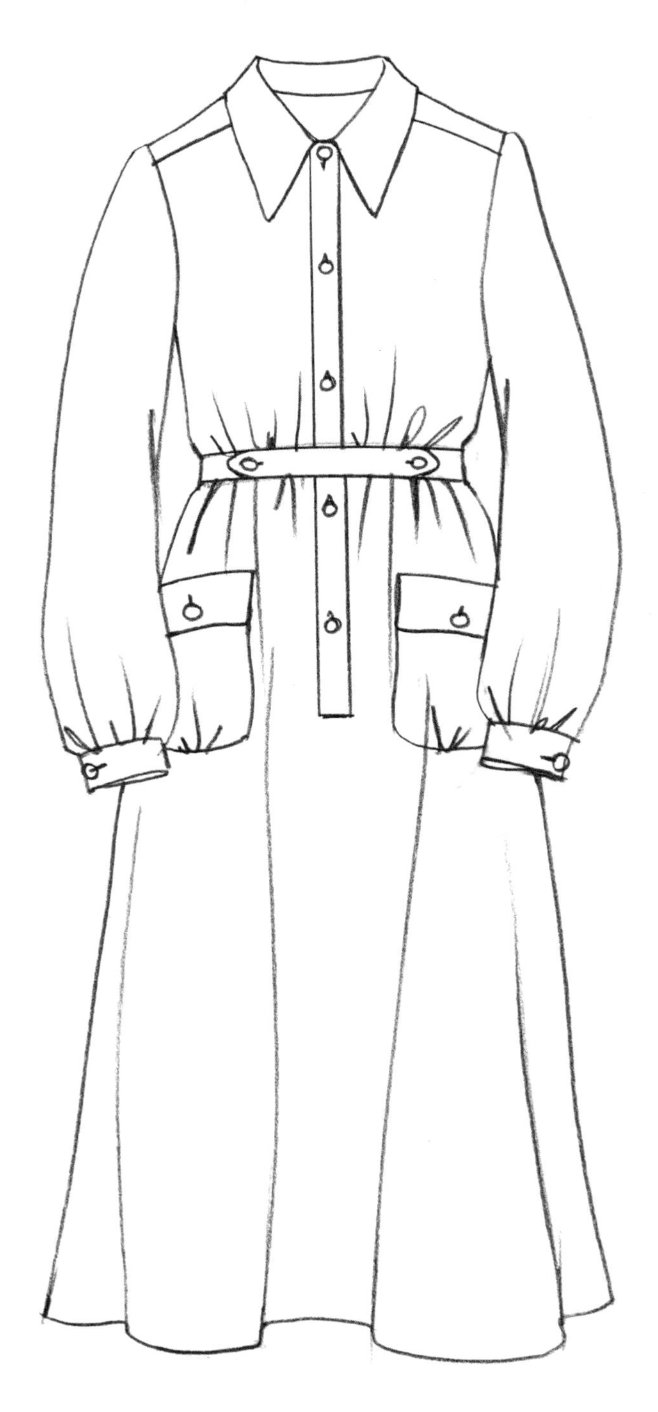

Uniform dress

“Peasant” dress

Dress with cowl neckline and 1930s batwing sleeves

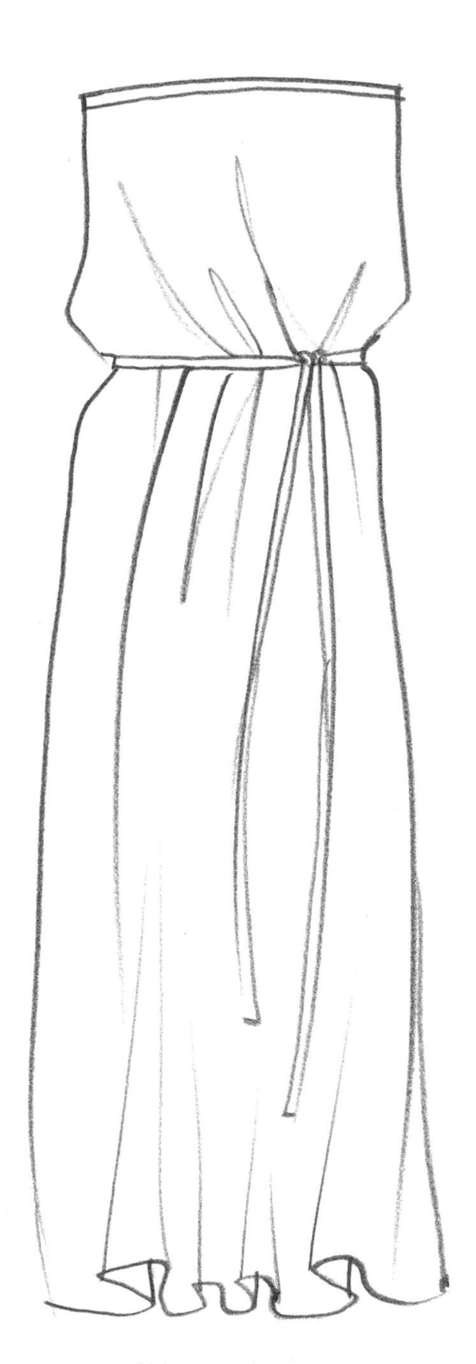

Halston strapless dress

1970s retro dress

Butterfly dress

Biba dress

Folk dress

One arm ruffled dress

Draped nightdress

Gypsy dress

Fine halter-neck dress

Halter neck with metal hoop

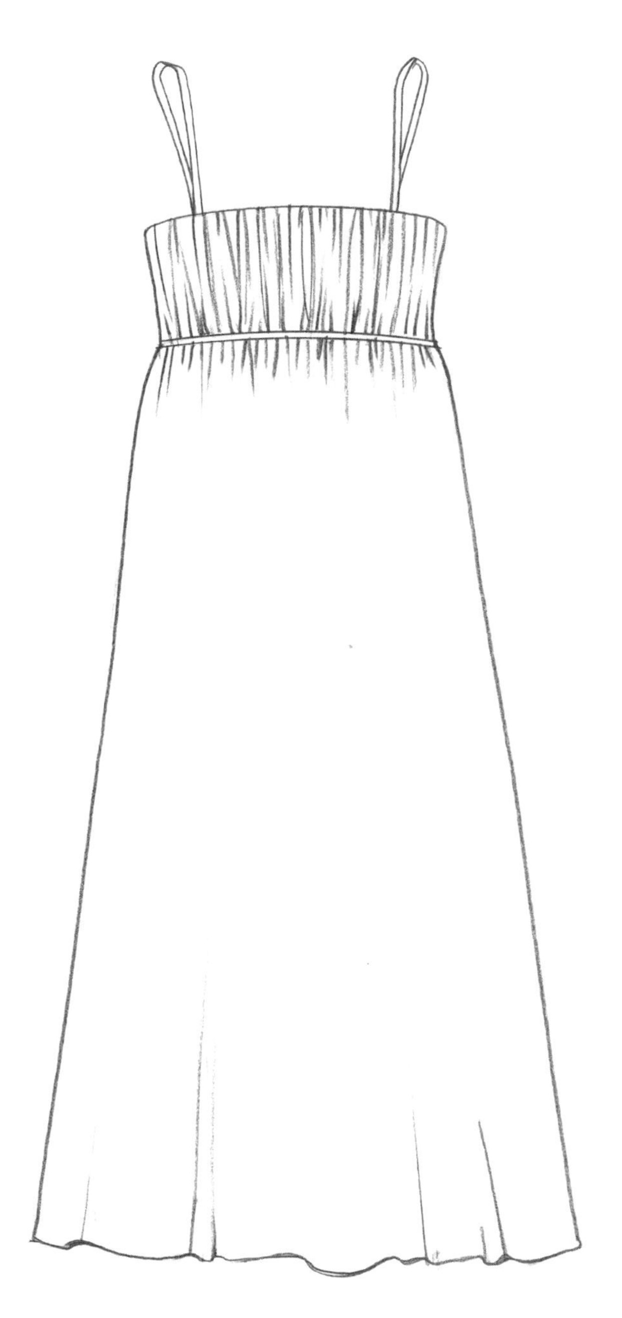

Empire dress

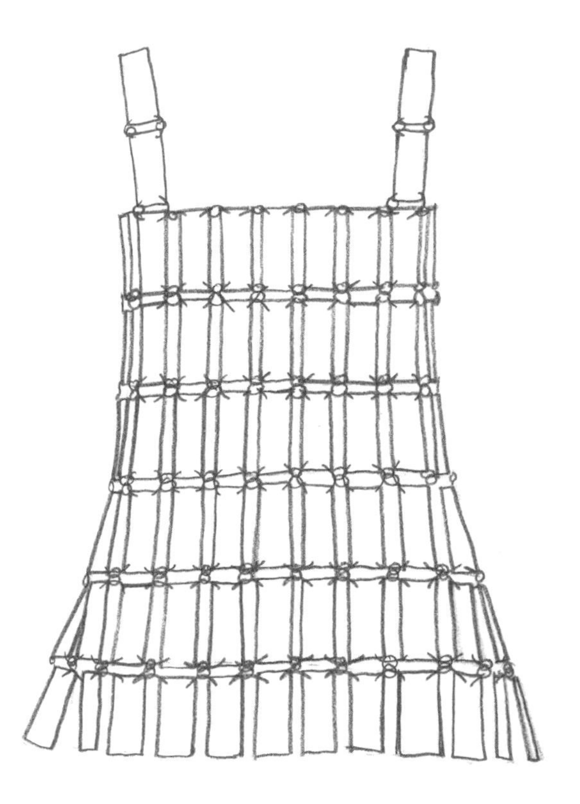

Chainmail dress

A-line dress

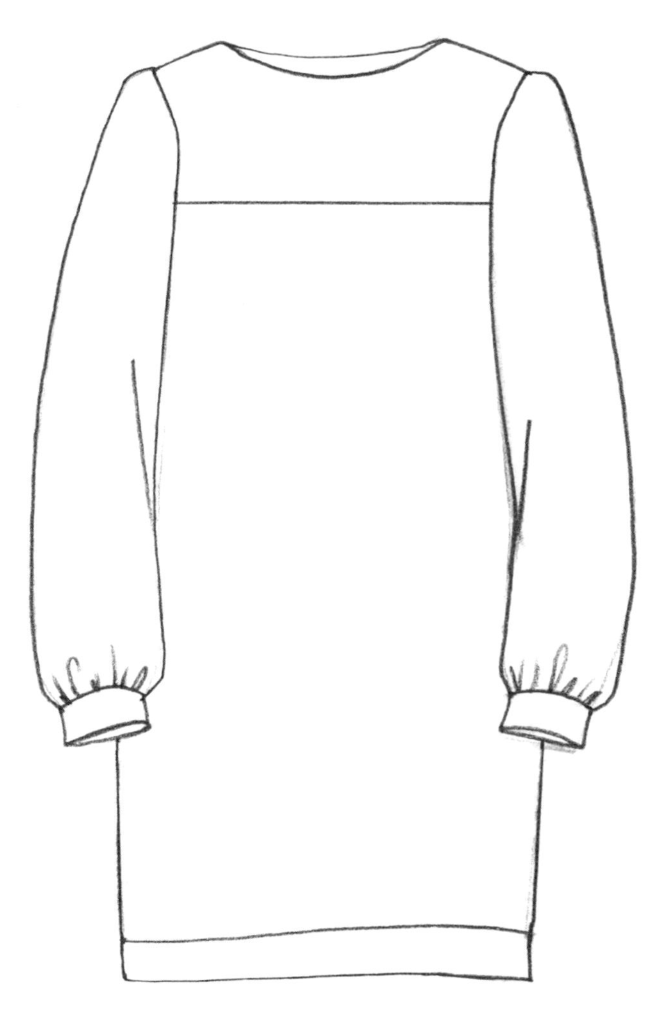

Sack dress

Cocktail dress

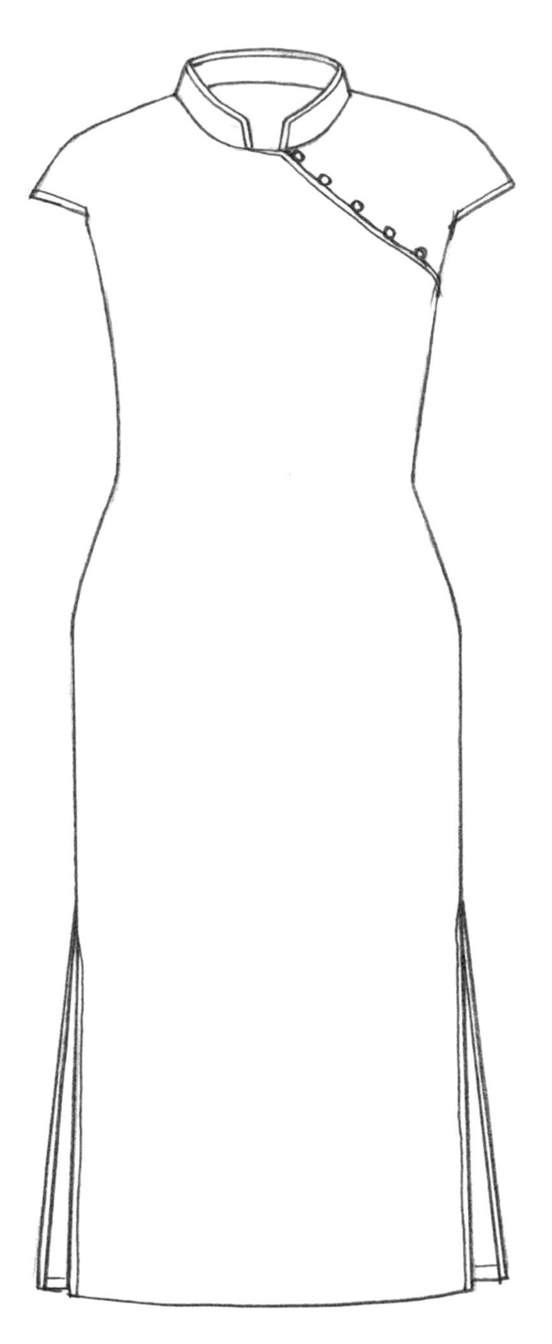

Chinese dress

1960s dress coat

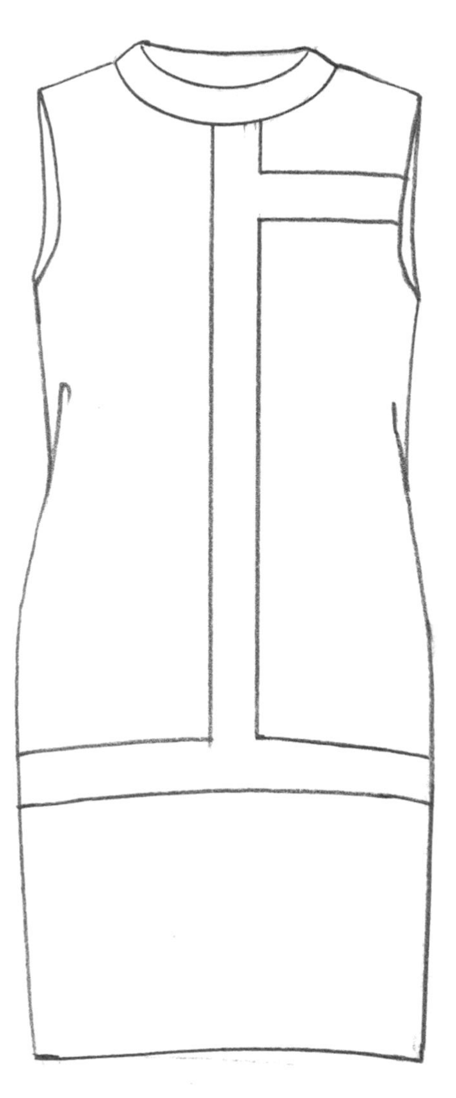

Straight dress with 1960s geometric print

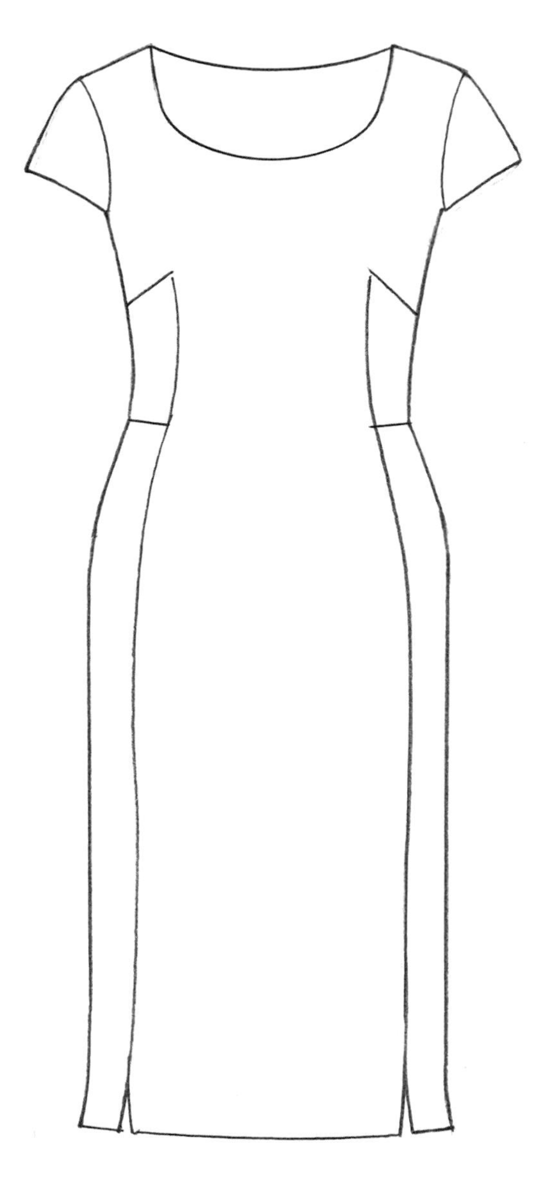
Little black dress

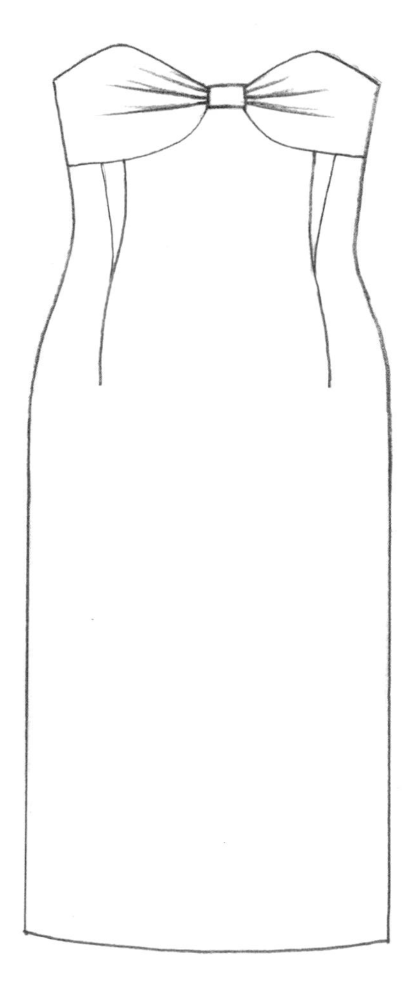
1950s bathing dress

1950s retro dress

Halter neck dress

"Sabrina" dress

"Marilyn" dress

Princess-line dress

Retro dress from beginning of twentieth century

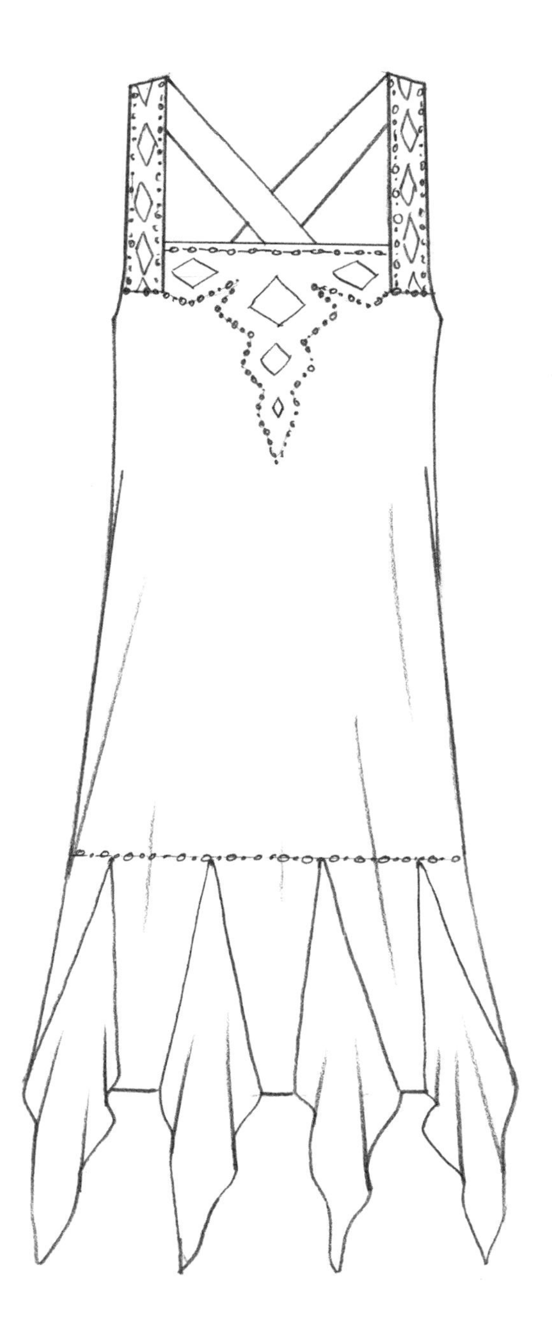

Charleston dress

Pants

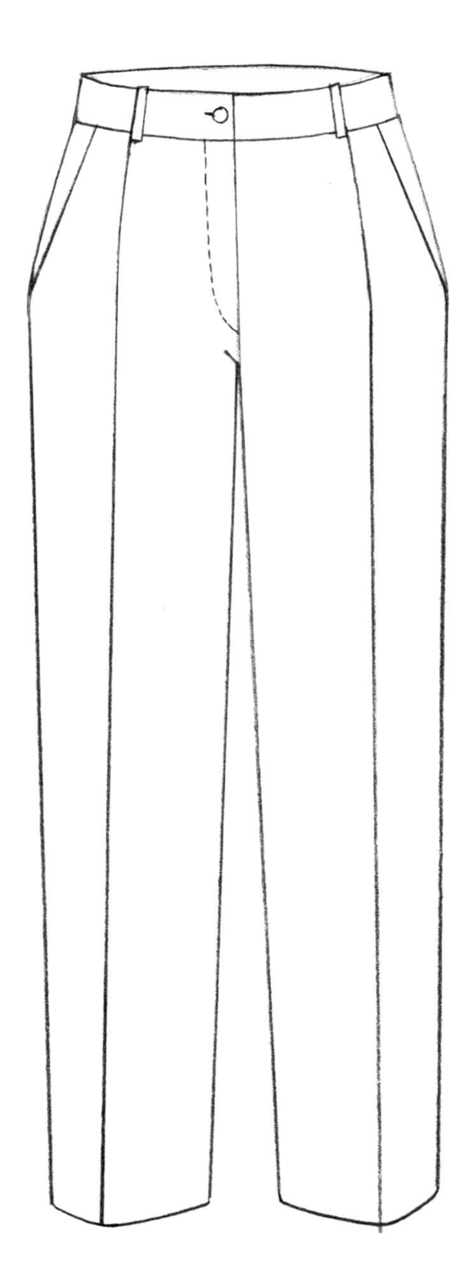

Classic pants, *front*

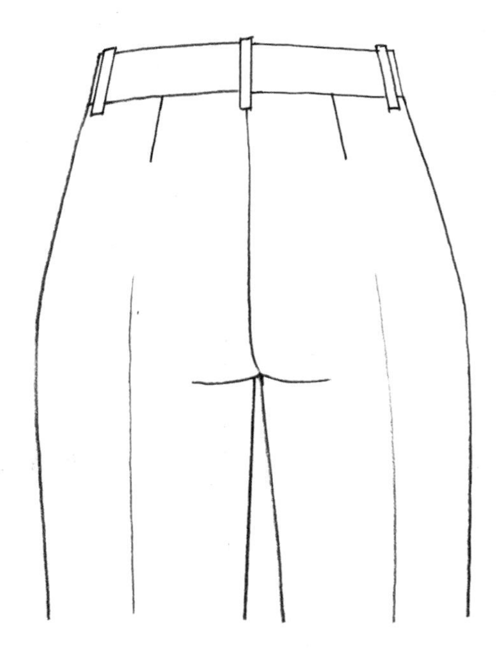

Classic pants, *back*

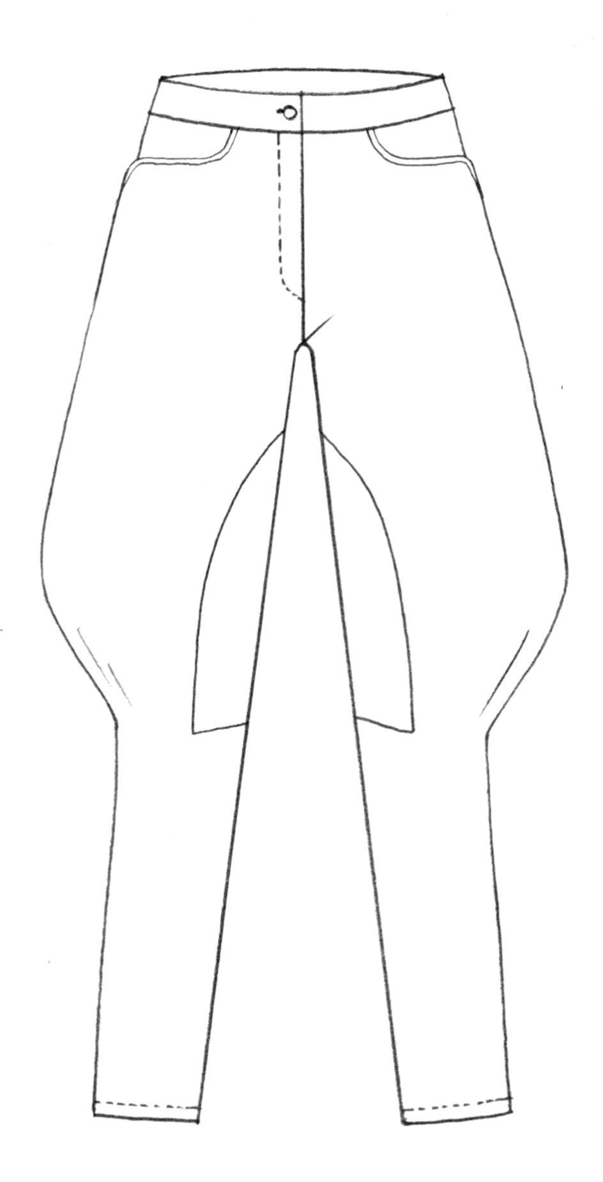

Jodhpur pants, *front*

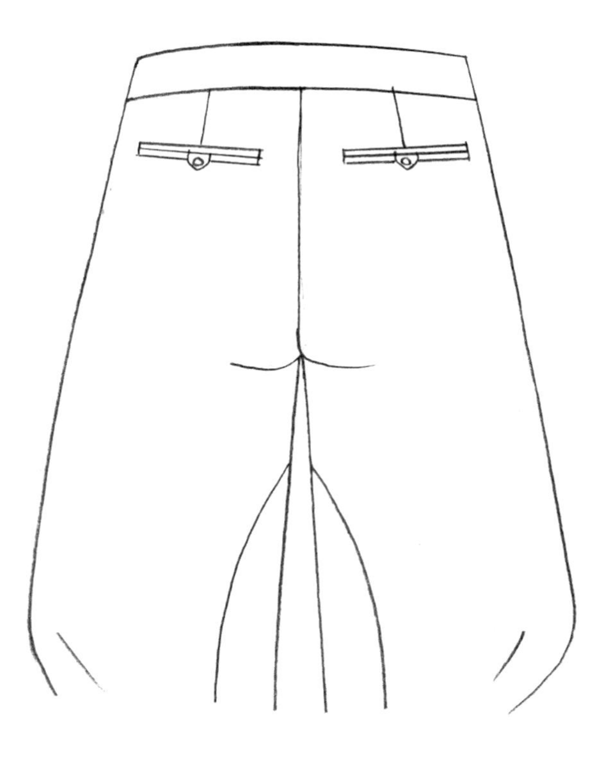

Jodhpur pants, *back*

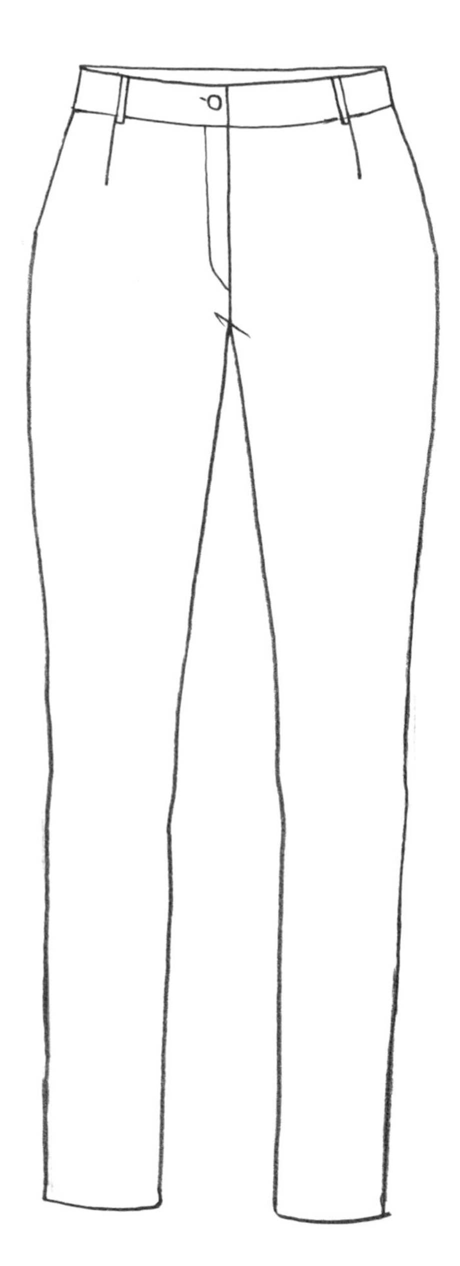

Fitted pants

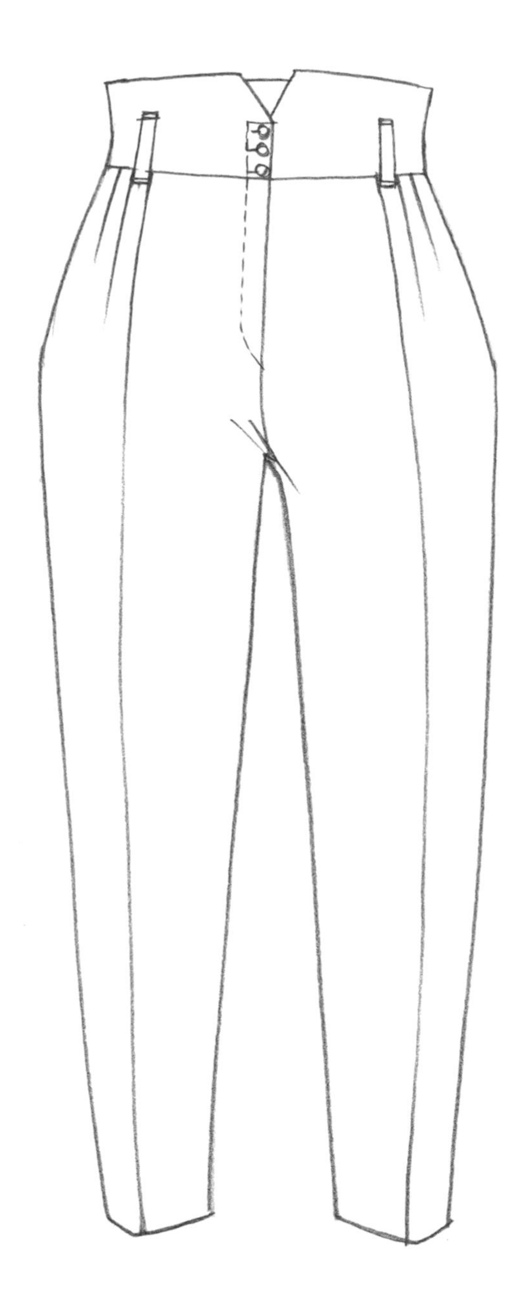

Bombacho pants

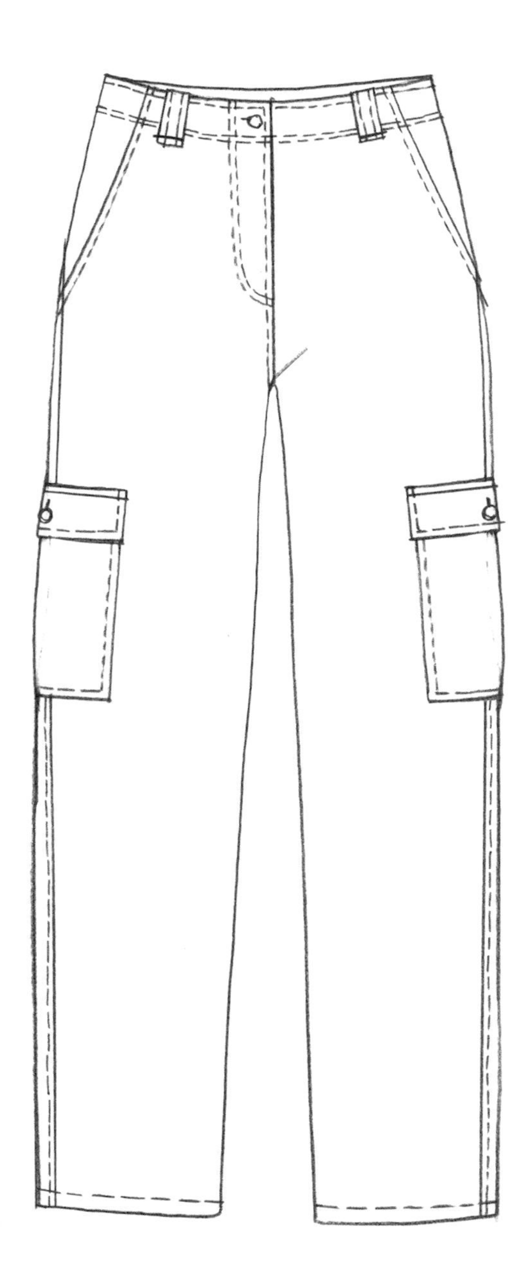

Cargo pants, *front*

Cargo pants, *back*

Bell-bottom pants

Baggy pants

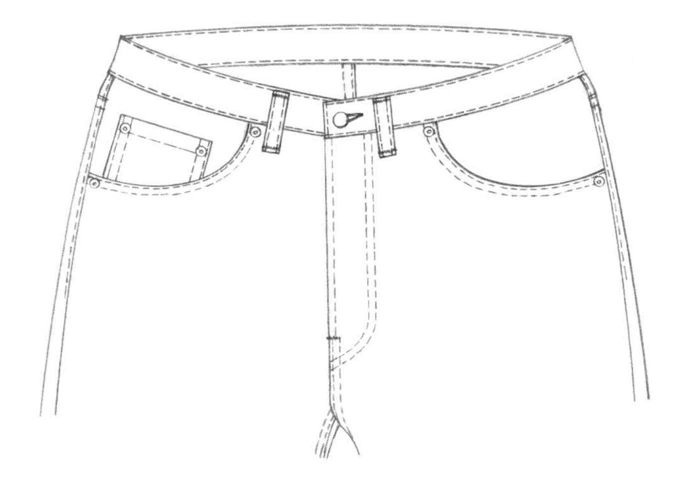

Detail high pants, *front*

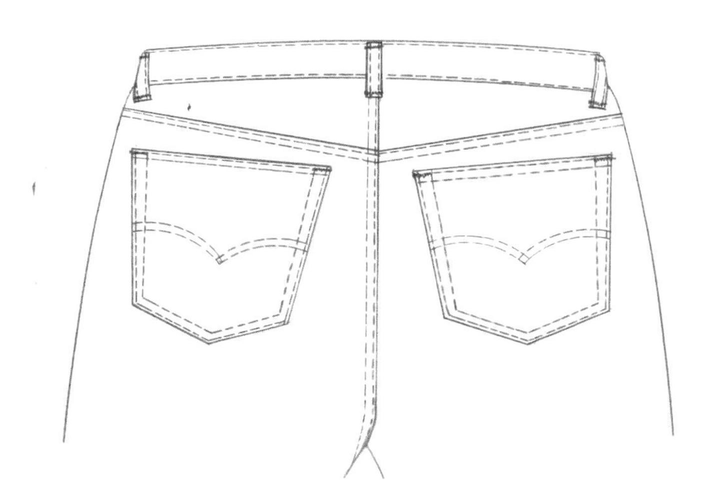

Detail high pants, *back*

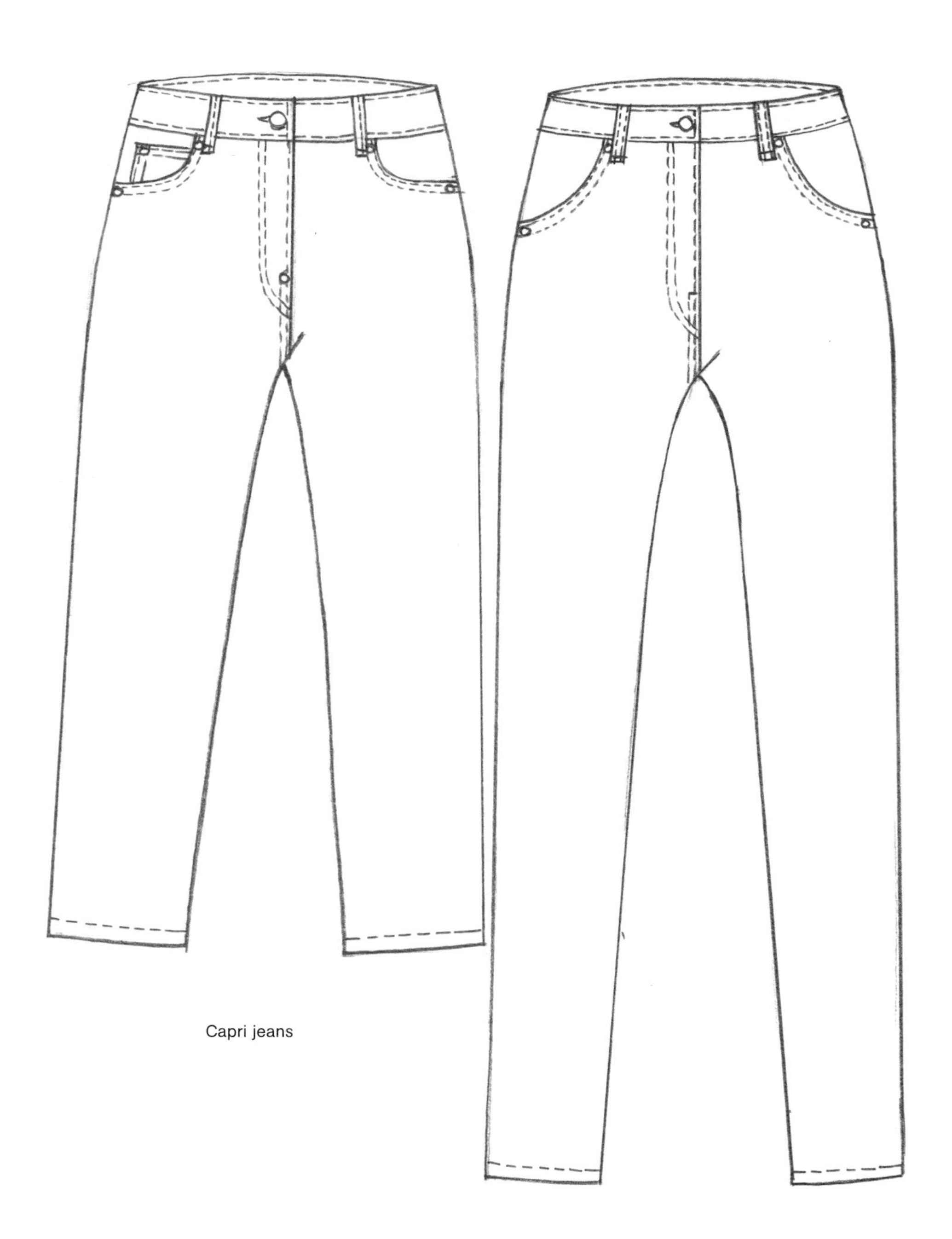

Capri jeans

Tight jeans

Wide jeans

Baggy jeans

Denim skirt

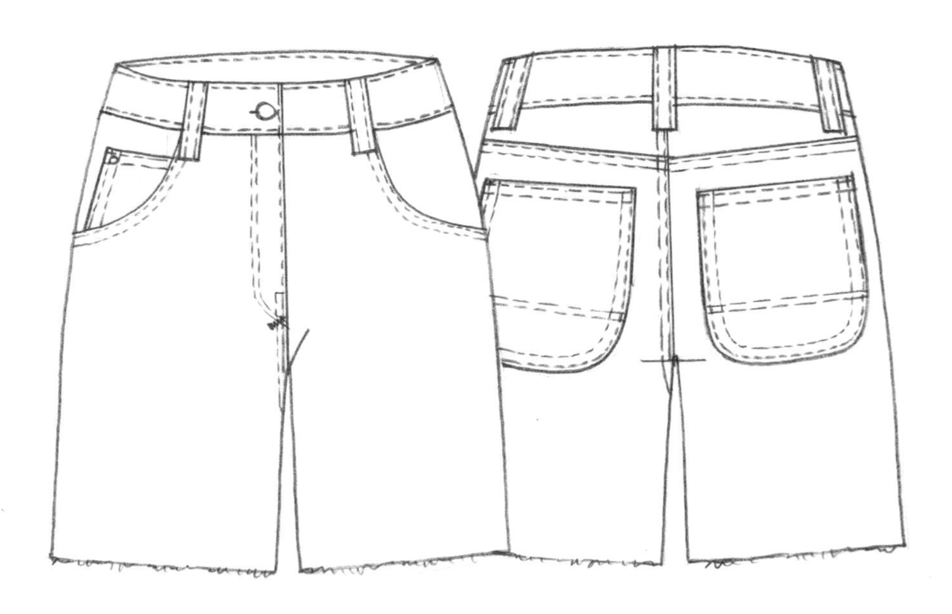

Denim Bermudas

Safari shorts

Samurai pants

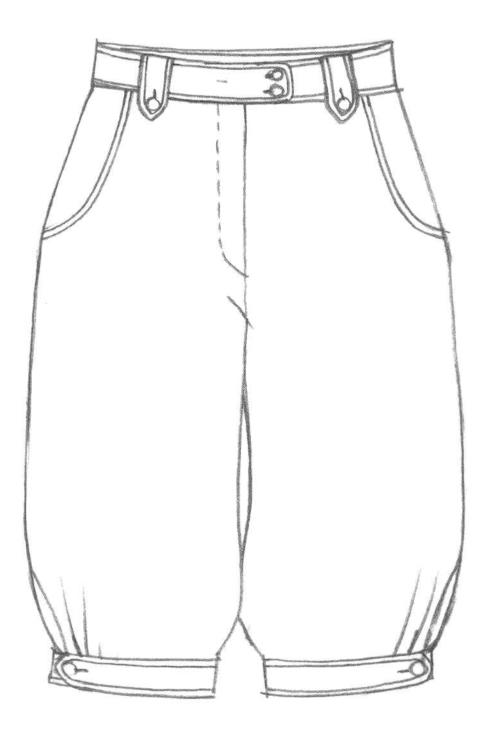

Knickers

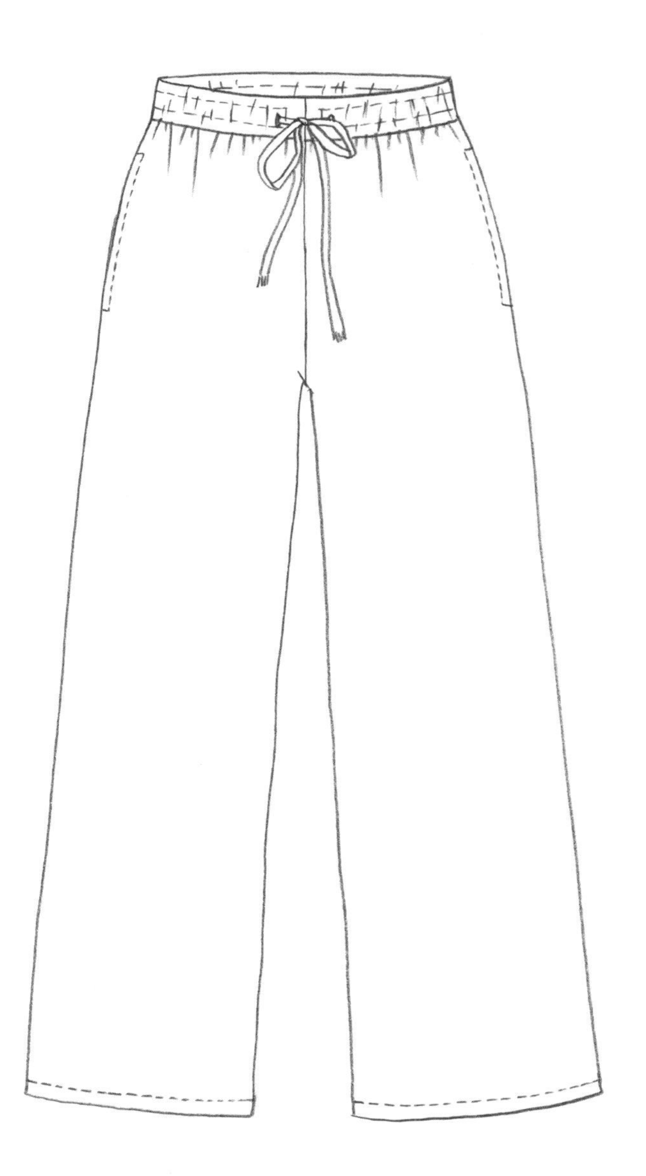

Pajama pants

Sweatpants

Retro shorts

1960s shorts

Poof shorts with tie

Shorts

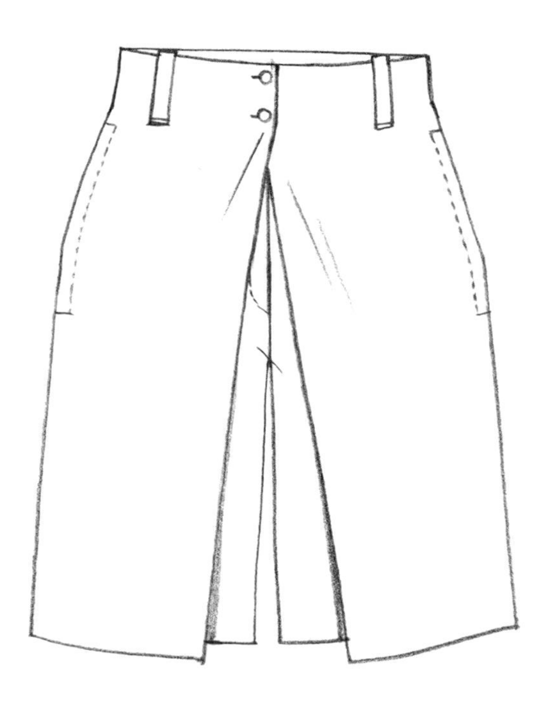

Apron pants

Bermudas

Cropped pants

Sarong pants

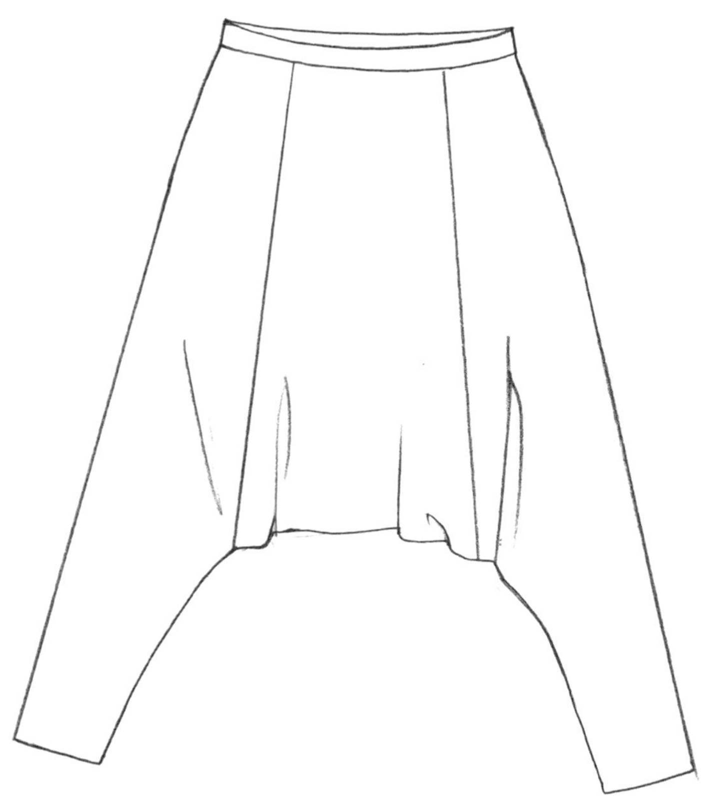

Saruel pants

Capri pants

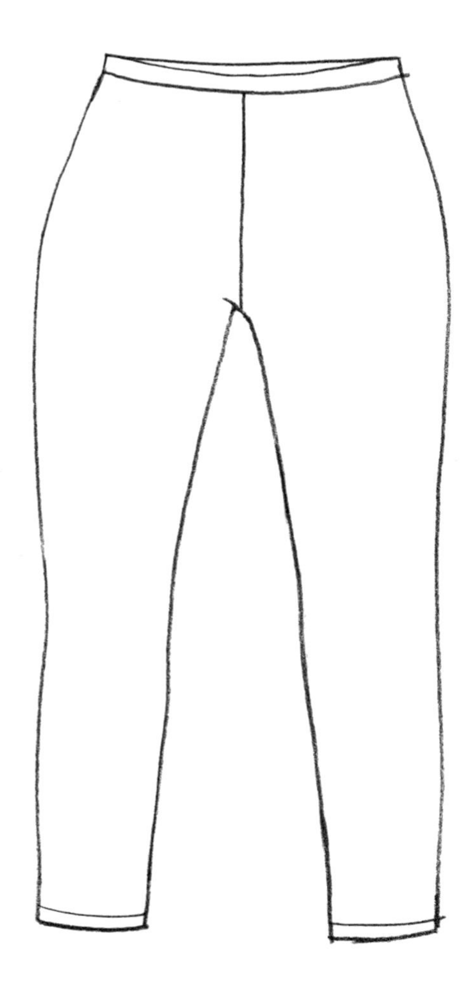

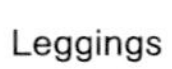

Leggings

Bombacho pants

1980s pants

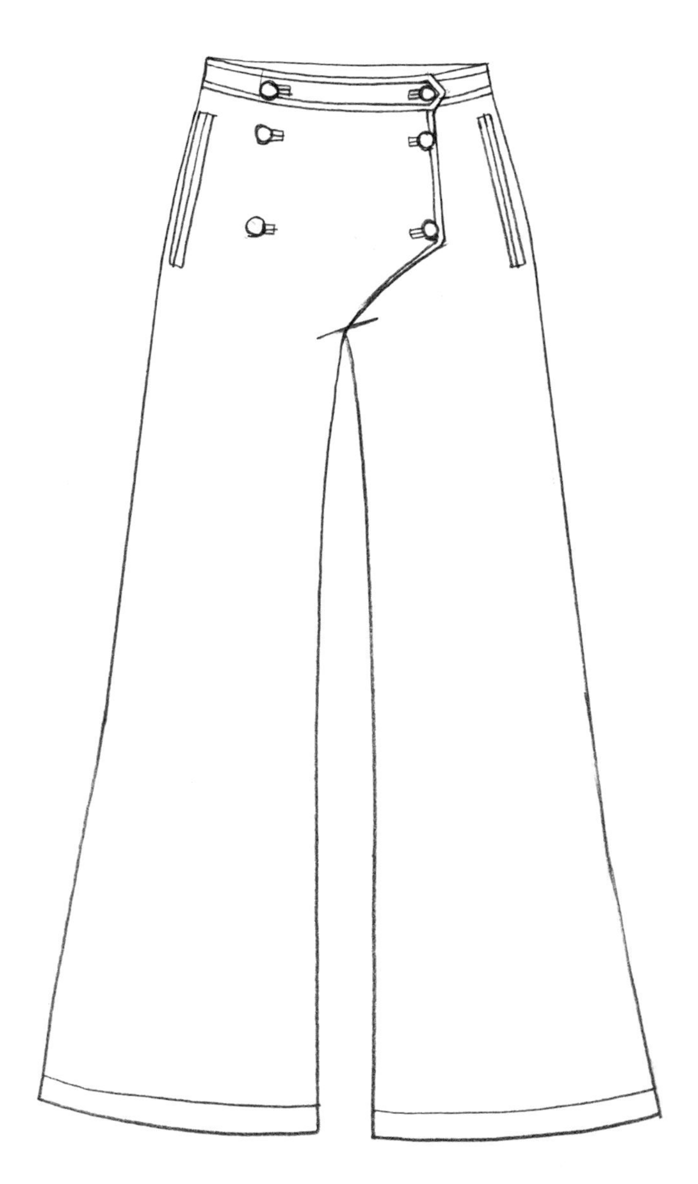

Marine-style pants

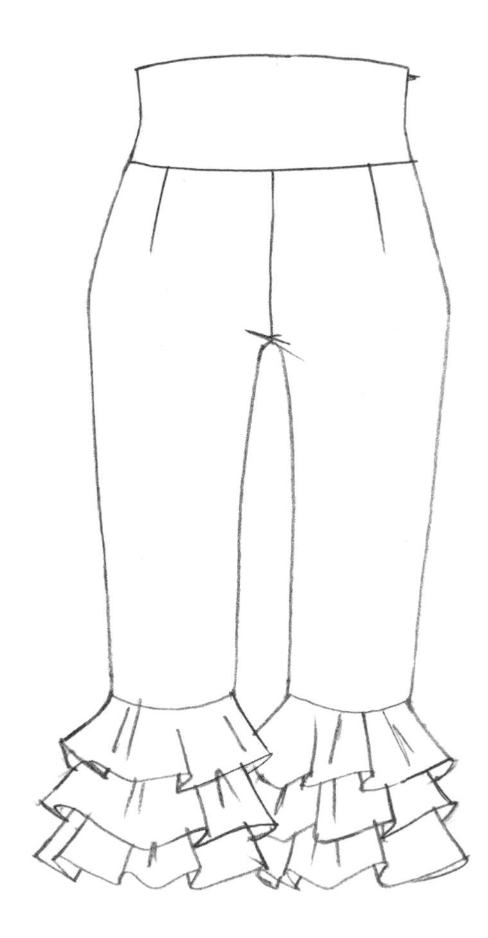

Carioca pants

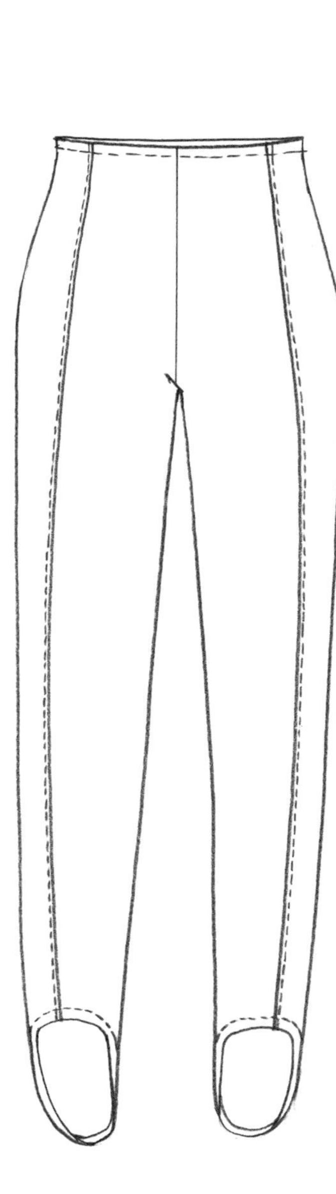

Fuseau ski pants

Halston jumpsuit

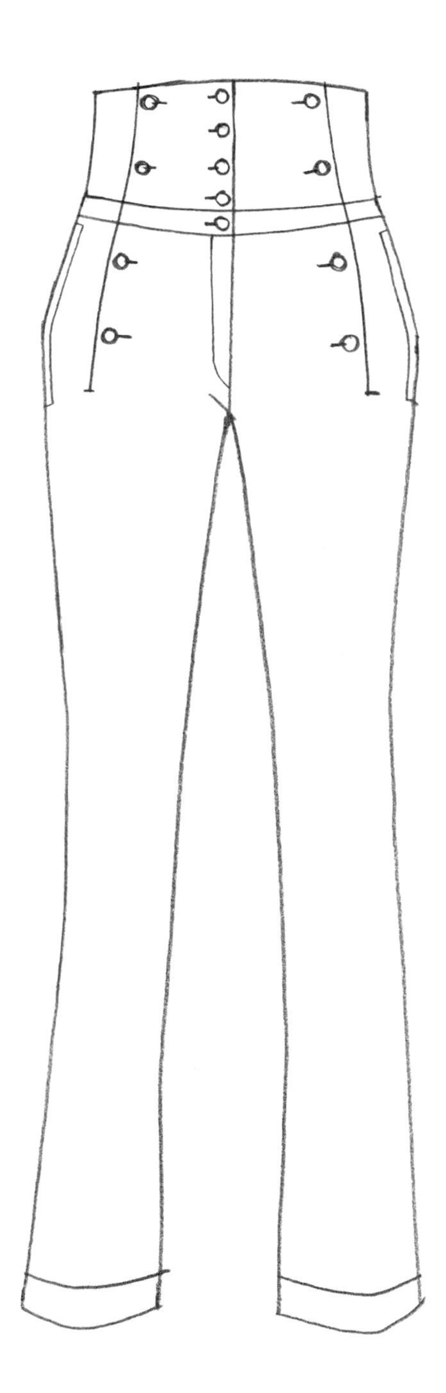

Cadet pants

1960s retro pants

Jackets & Coats

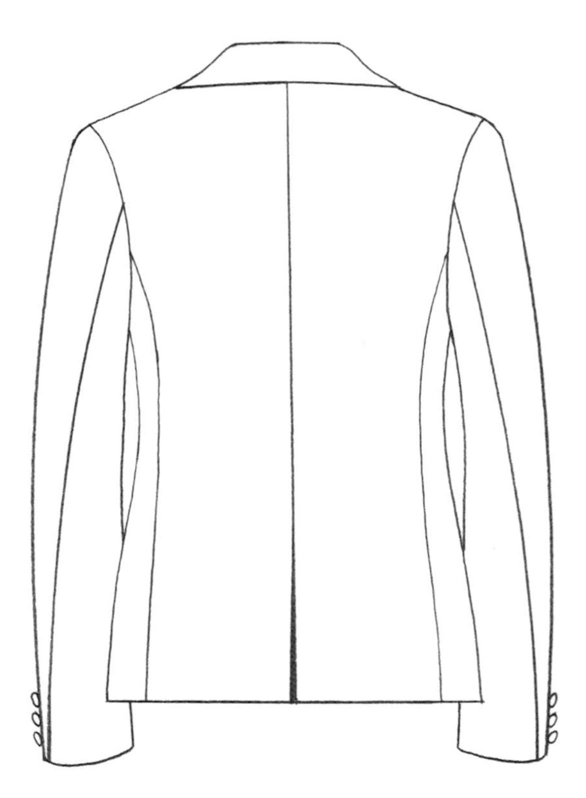

Tailored jacket, *back*

Tailored jacket, *profile*

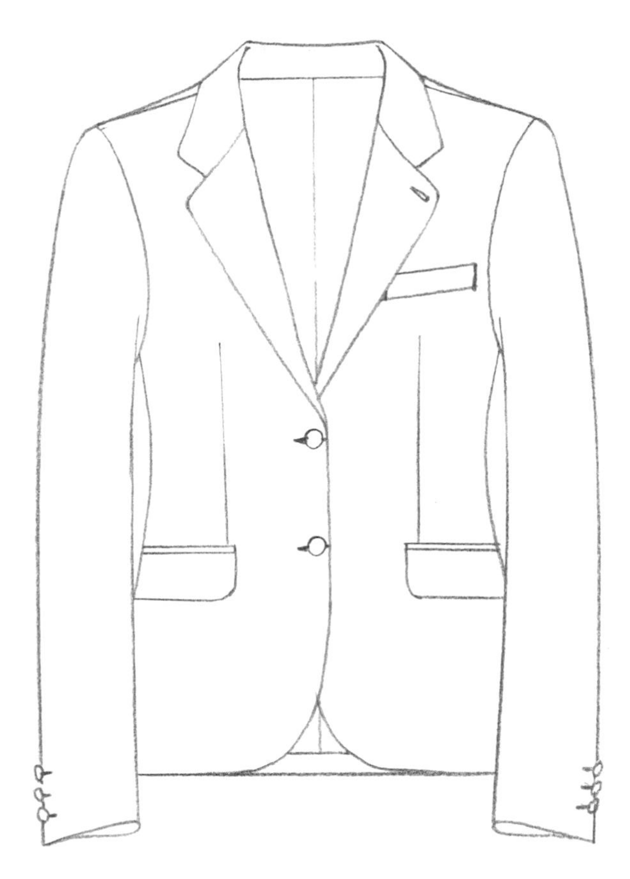

Tailored jacket, *front*

Blazer, *front*

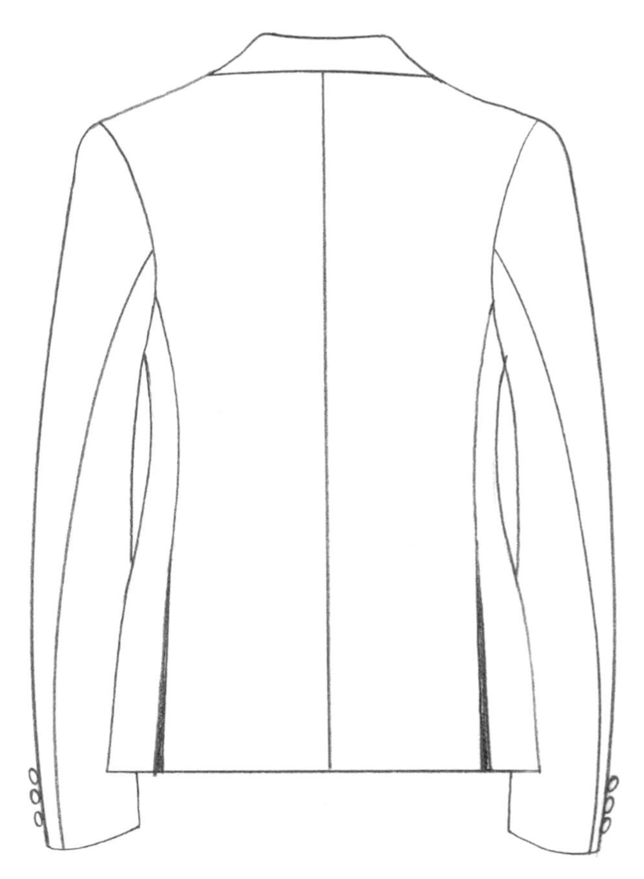

Blazer, *back*

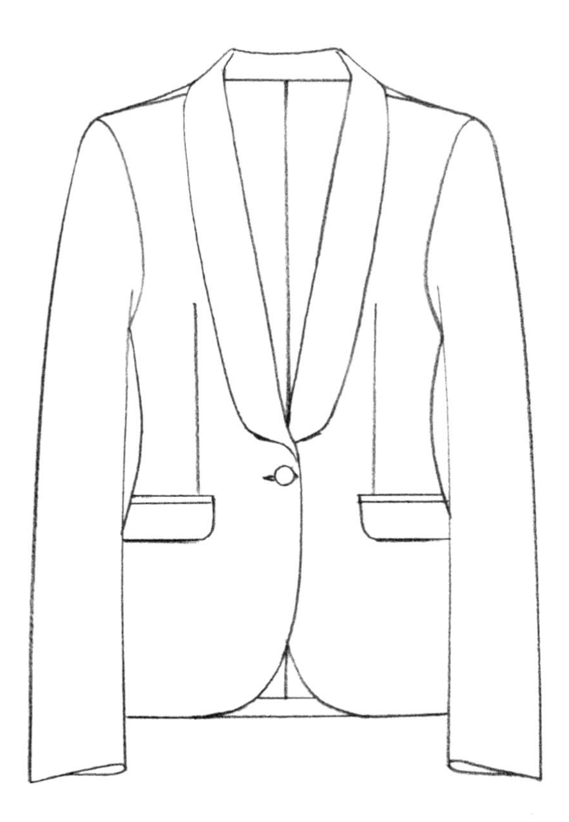

Dinner jacket

Spencer jacket

Bolero jacket

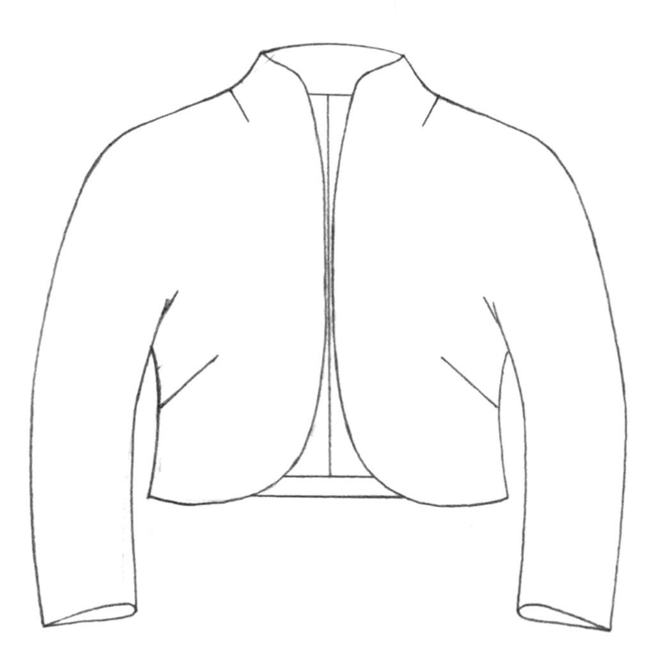

Bolero jacket with Japanese sleeve

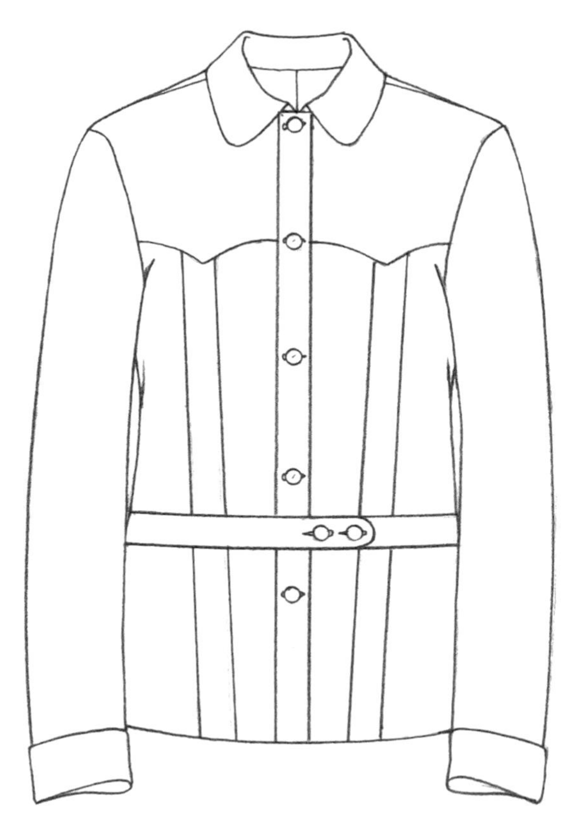

Hunting jacket

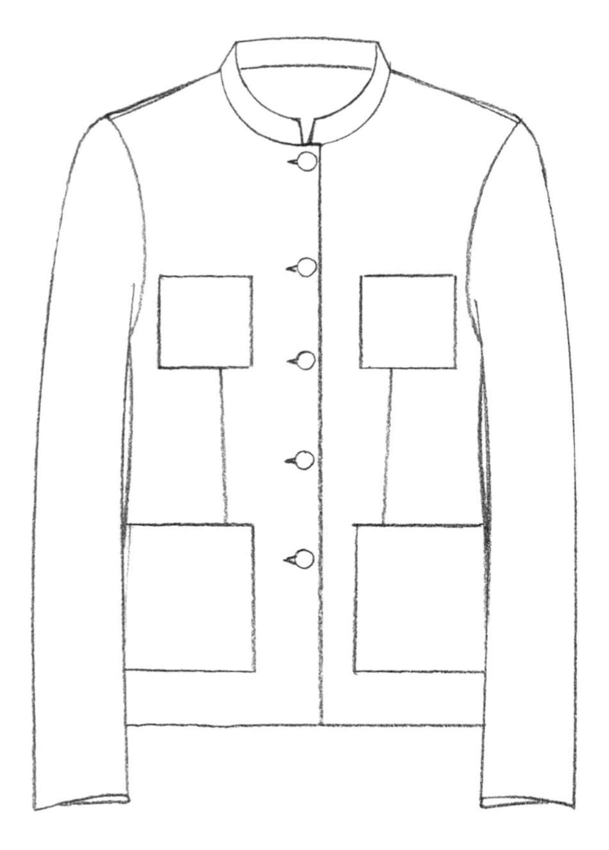

Mao-style jacket

Waistcoat for tailcoat

Waistcoat, *front*

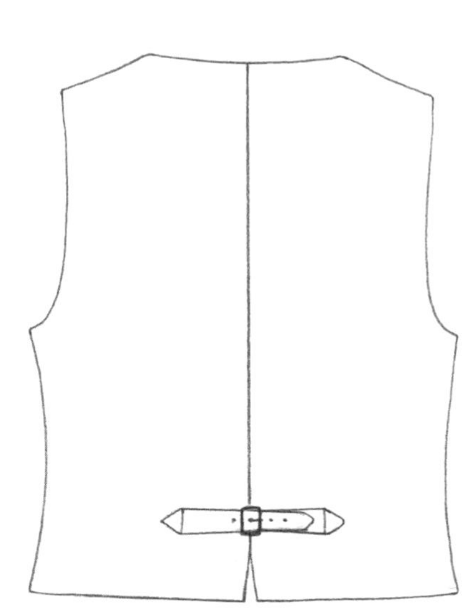

Waistcoat, *back*

Tailcoat

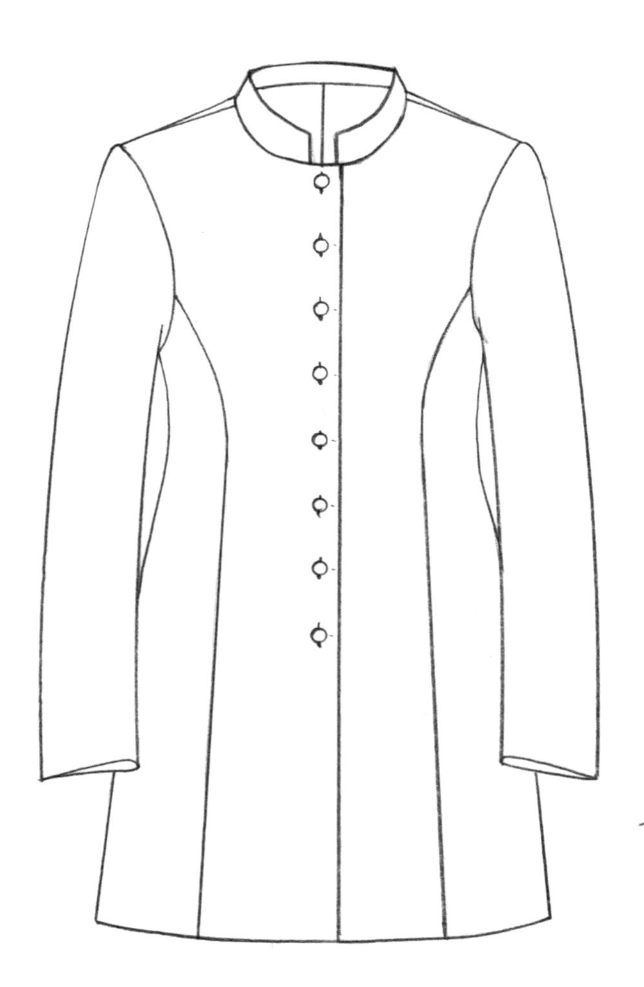

Frock coat with Mao-style collar

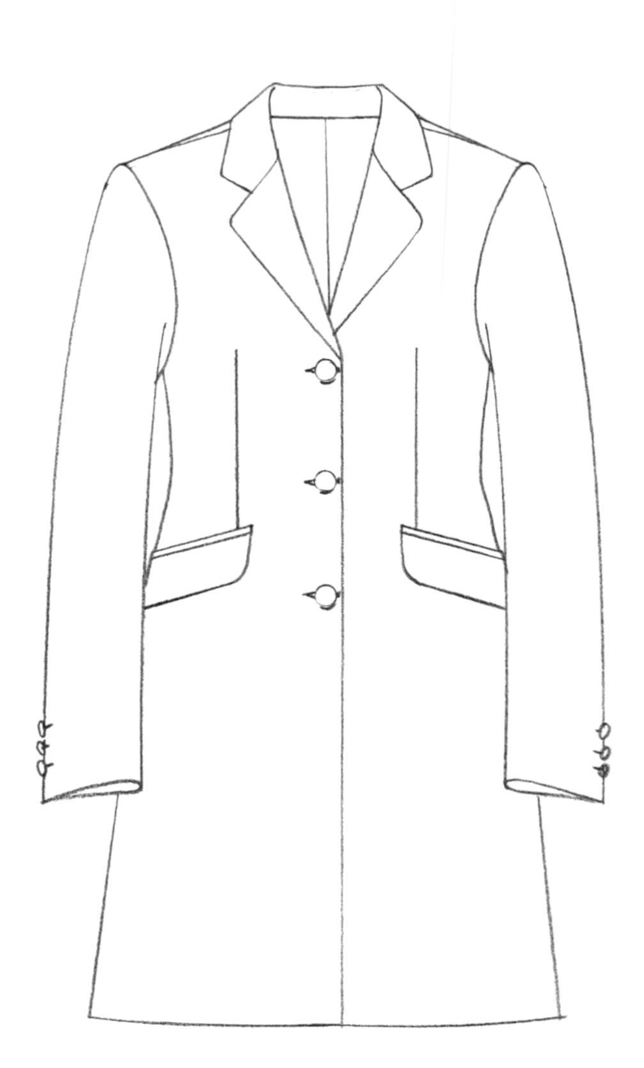

Frock coat

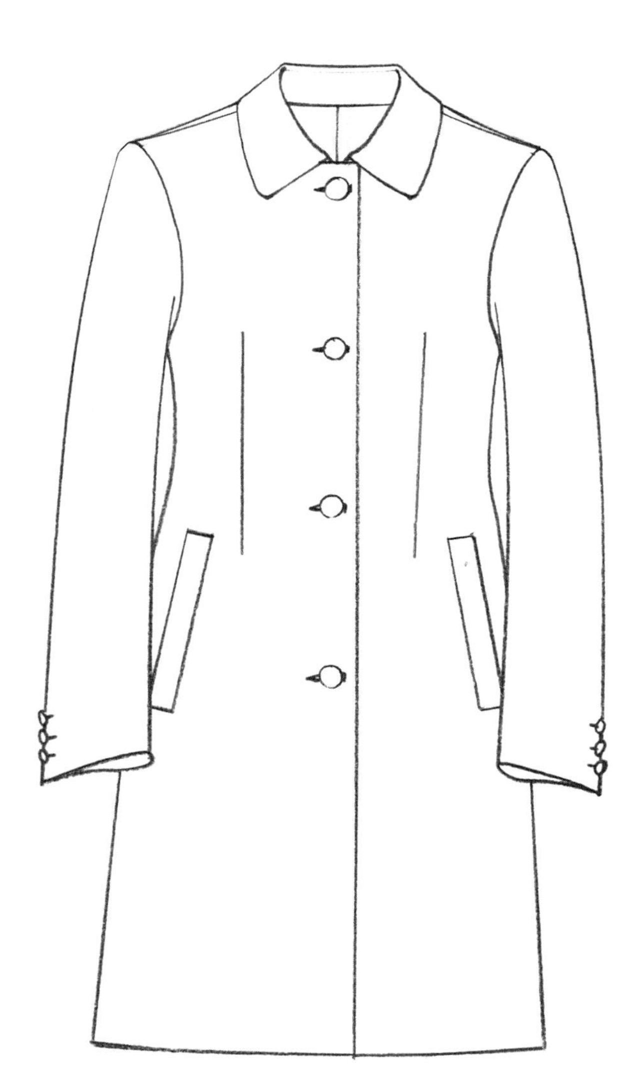

Smart coat

Marine-style coat

Classic coat, *front*

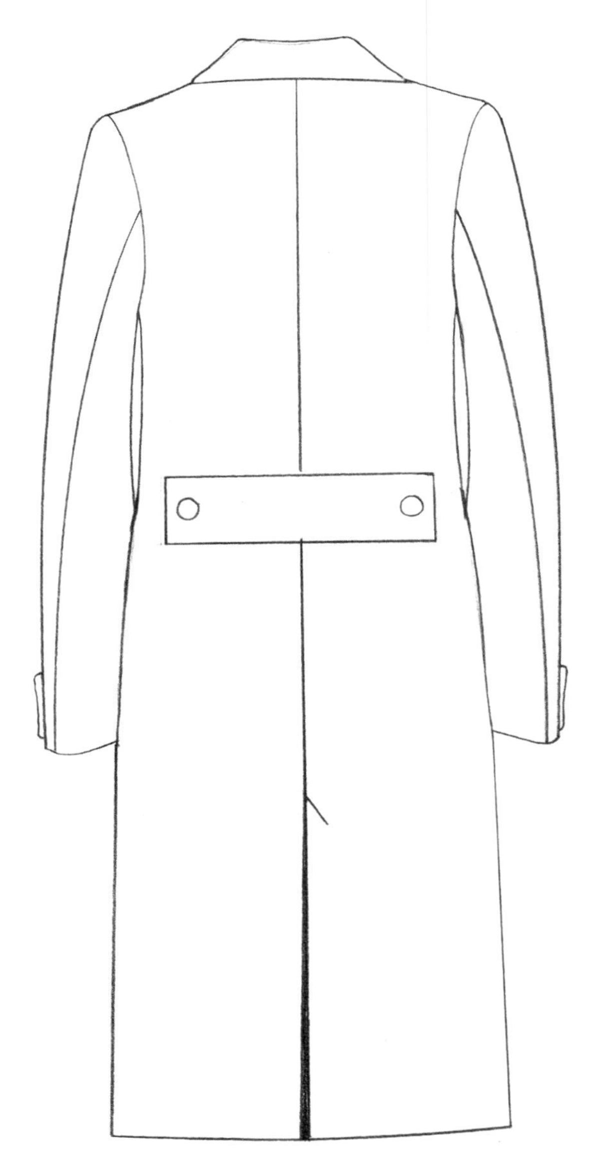

Classic coat, *back*

Minimalist coat, *front*

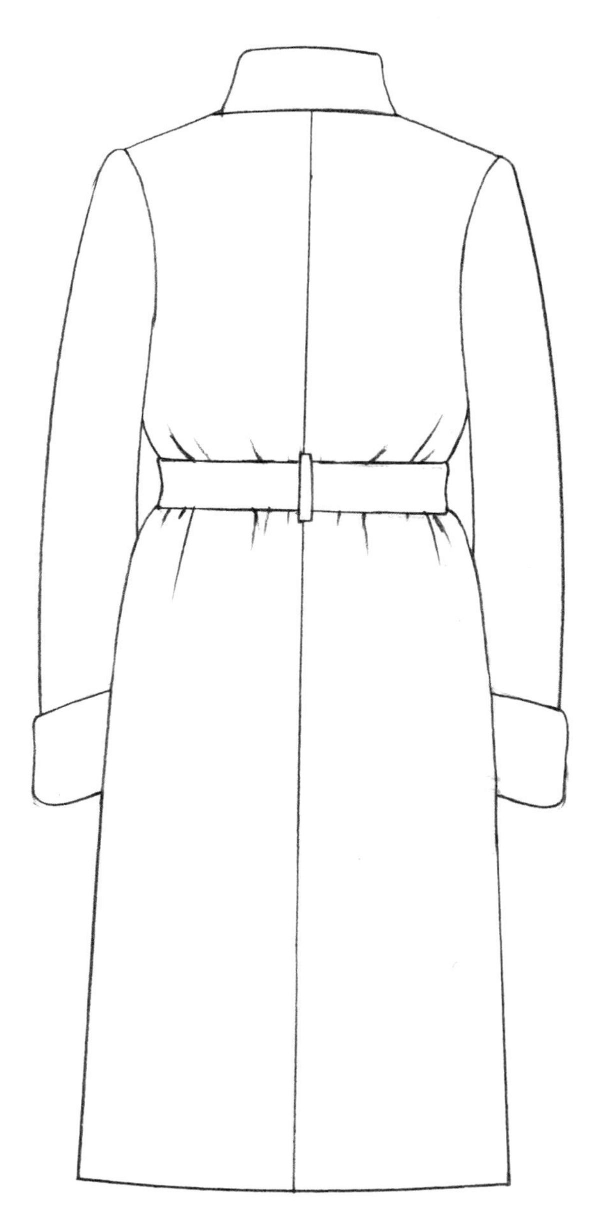

Minimalist coat, *back*

Trench coat, *front*

Trench coat, *back*

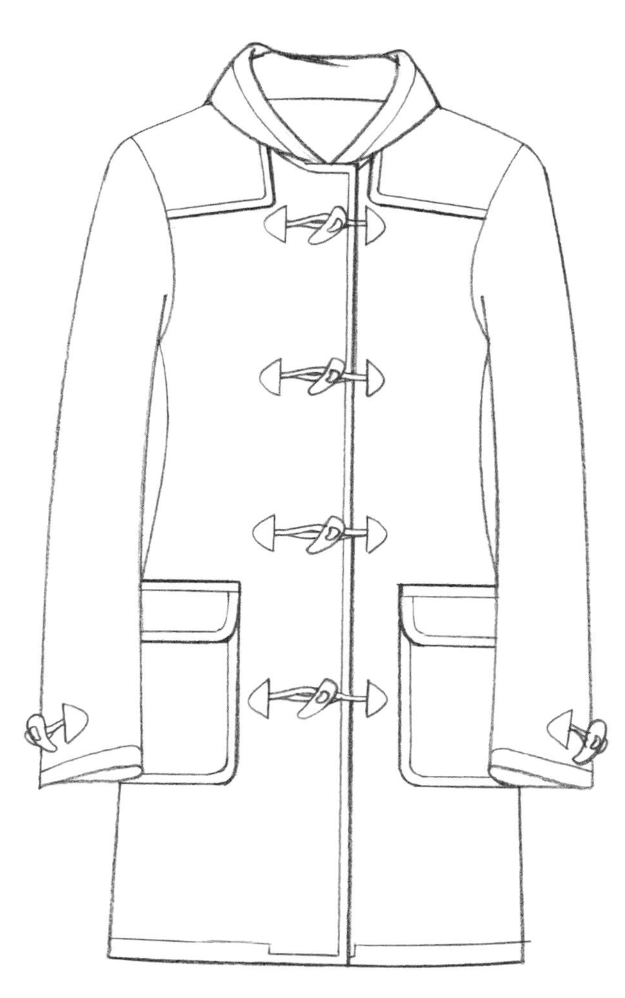
Montgomery jacket, *front*

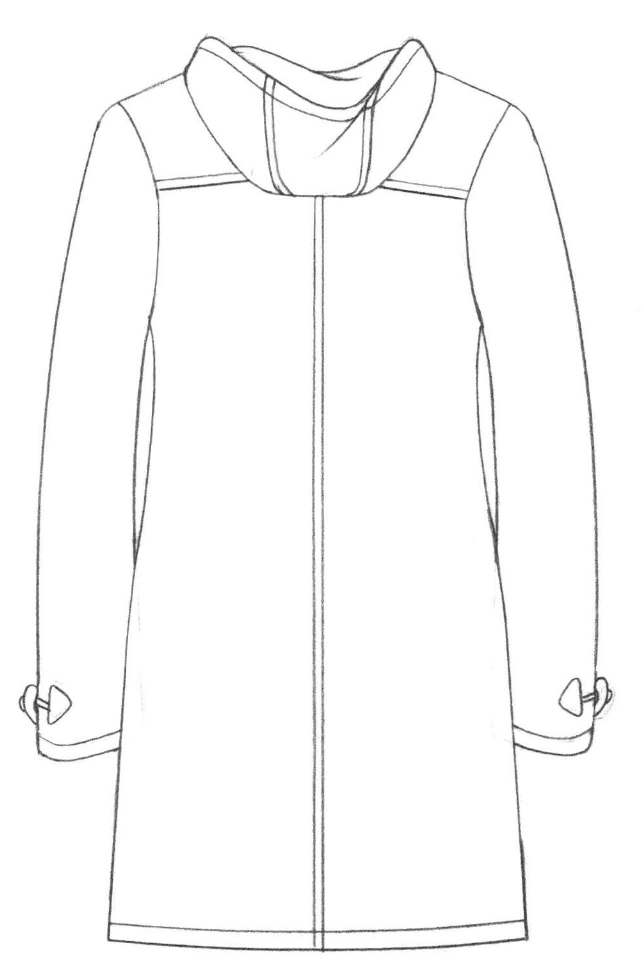
Montgomery jacket, *back*

A-line coat

Raincoat

Balloon coat

Retro-style coat

Flared coat

Bomber jacket

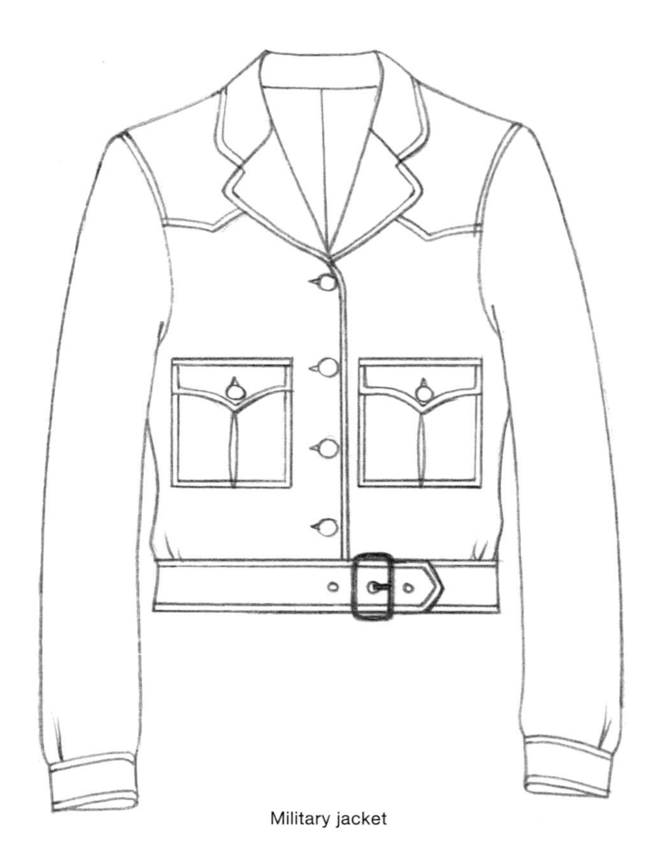

Military jacket

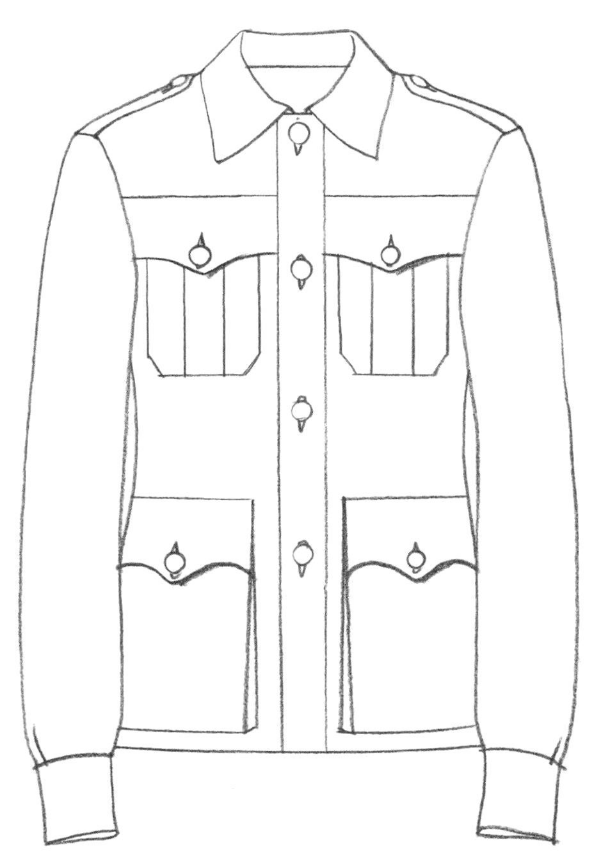

Safari jacket, *front*

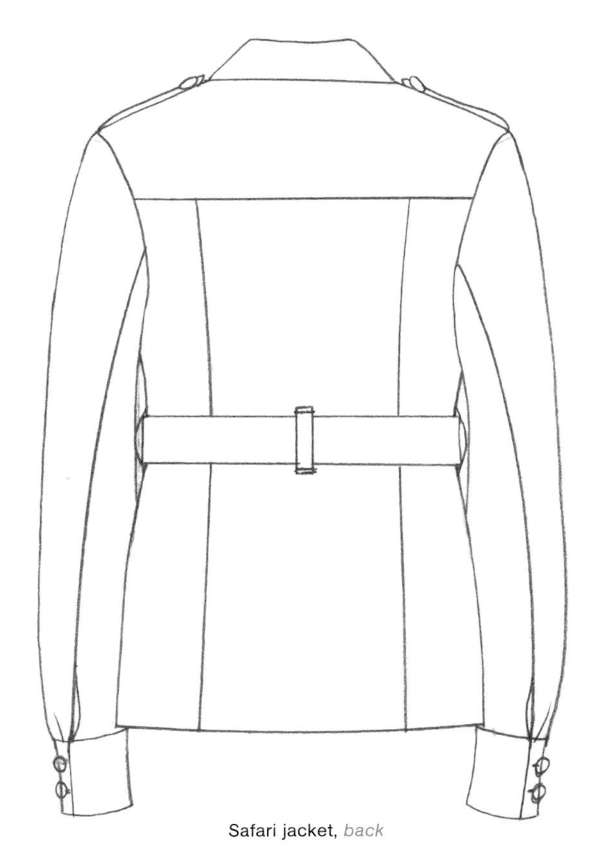

Safari jacket, *back*

Leather bomber jacket

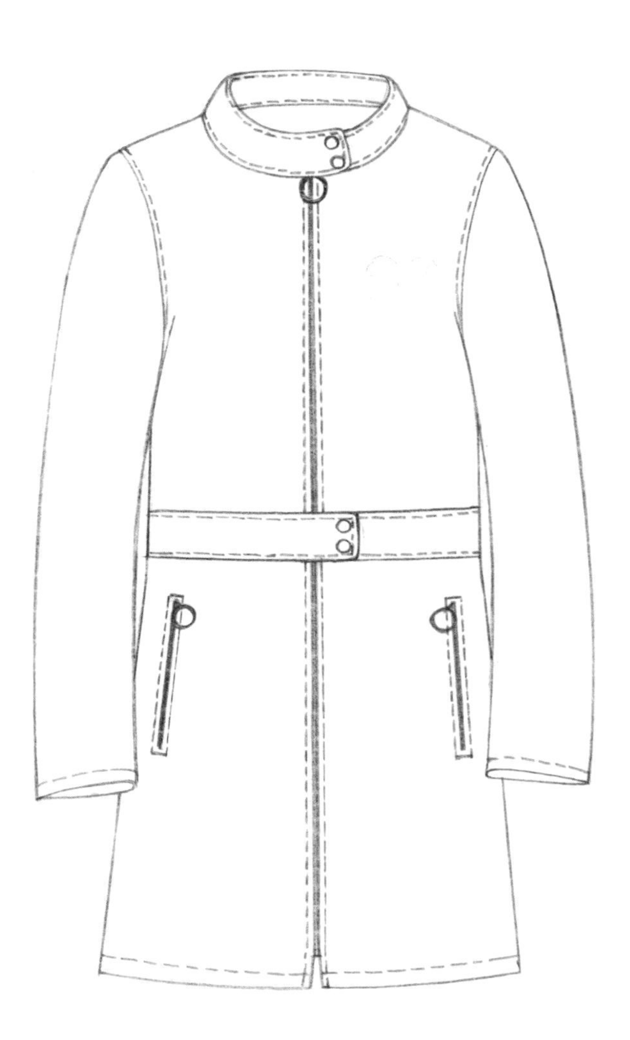

Patent leather 1960s coat

Baseball jacket

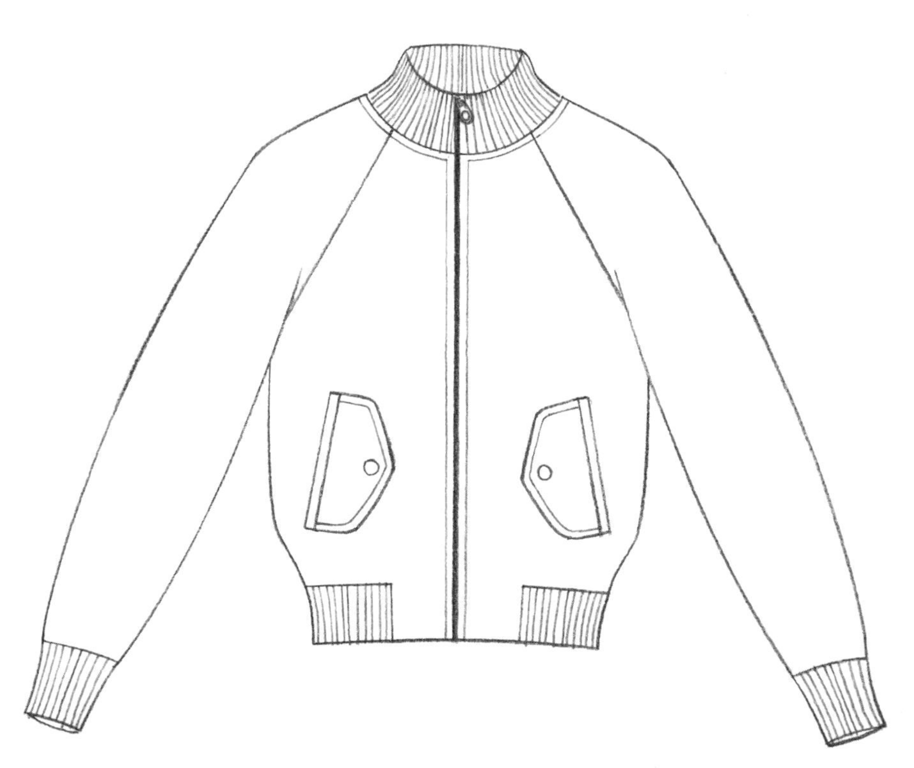
Bomber jacket

Barbour jacket

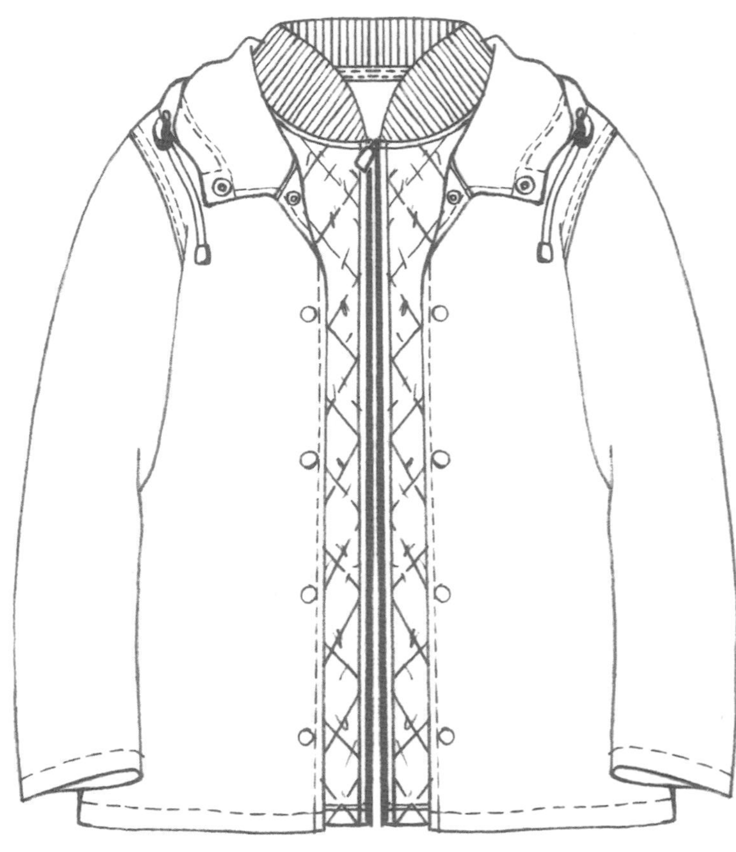

Double parka

Barbour quilted jacket

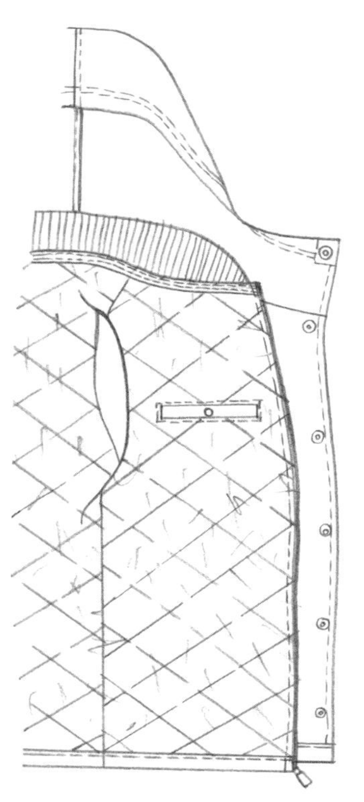

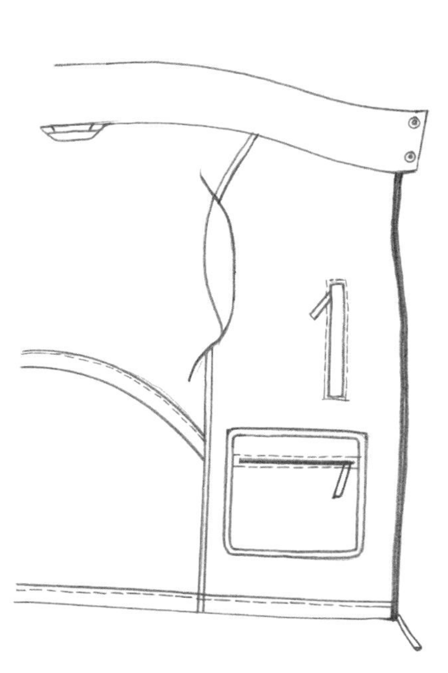
Parka insides

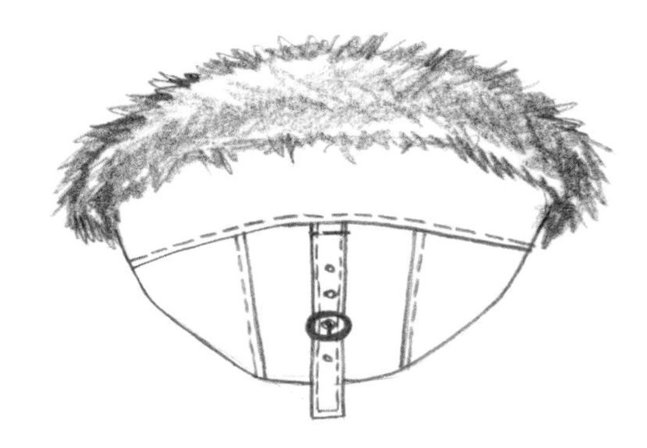

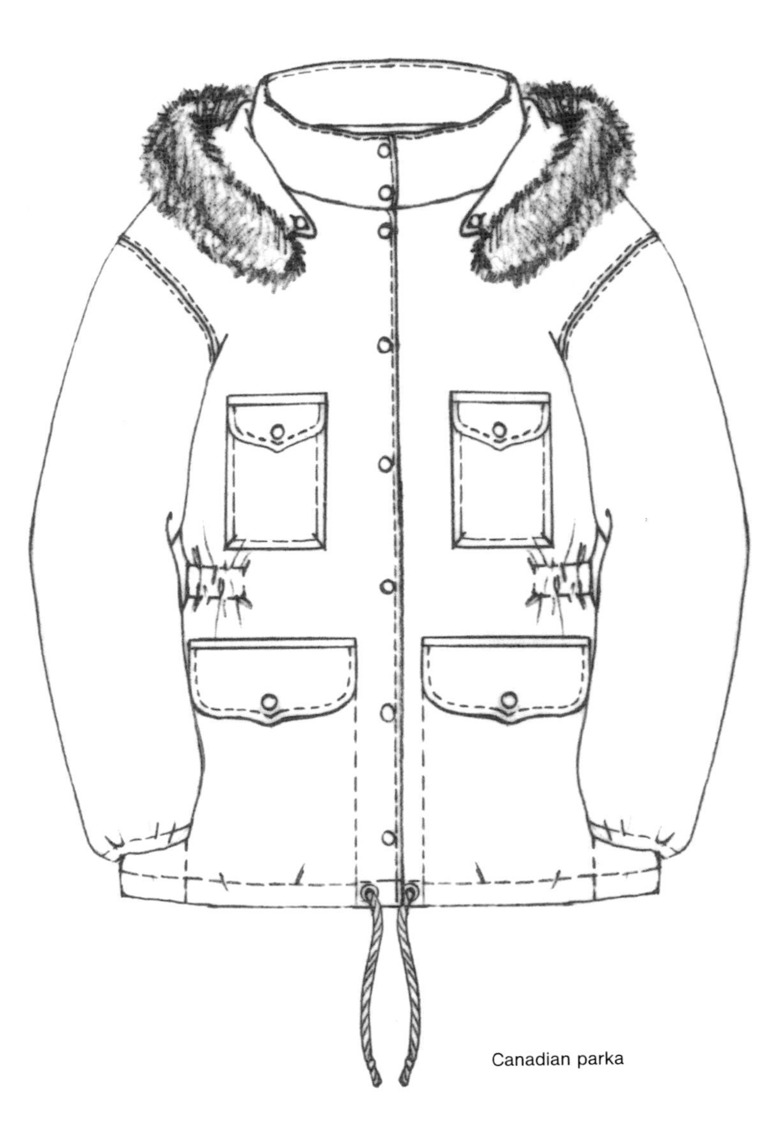

Canadian parka

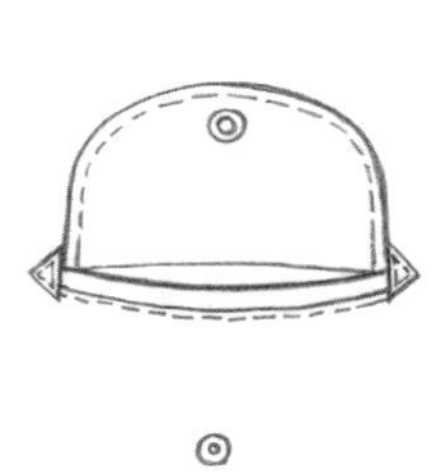

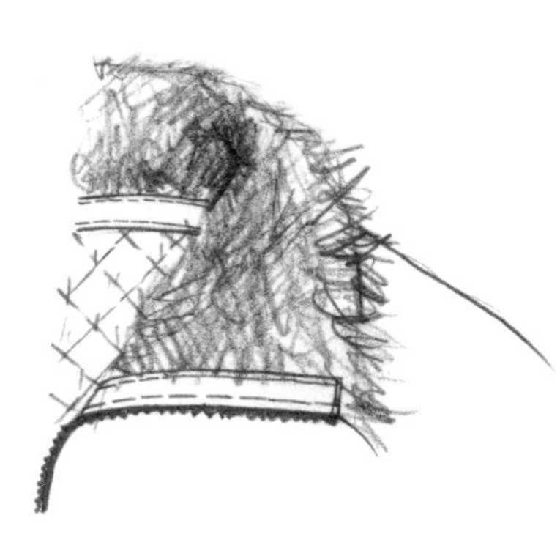

Parka details: hood, collar and pocket

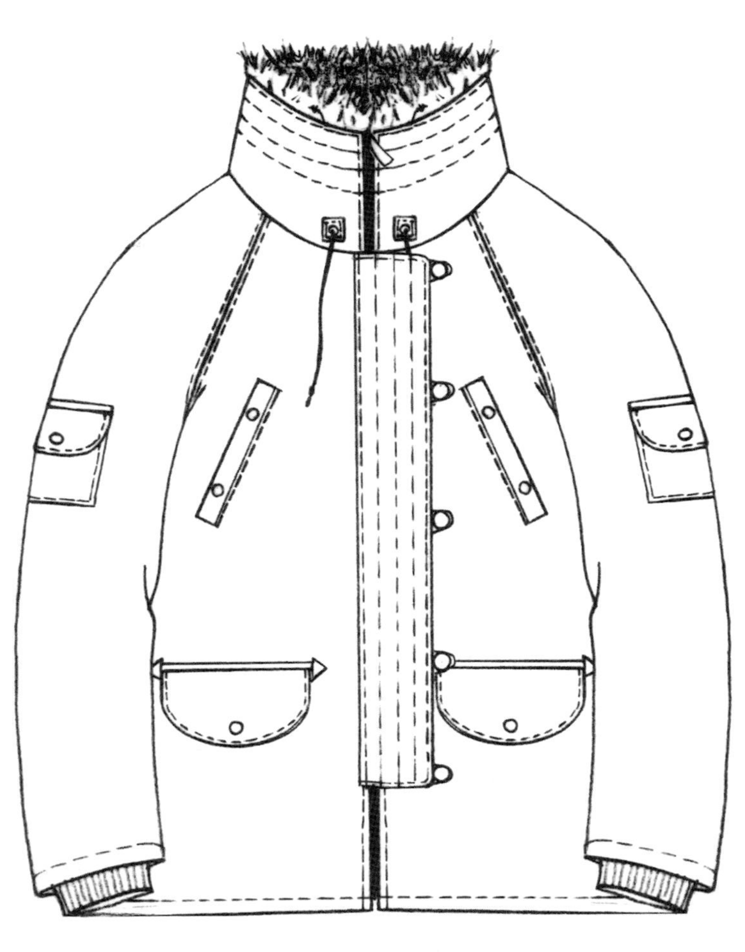
Fur-lined parka

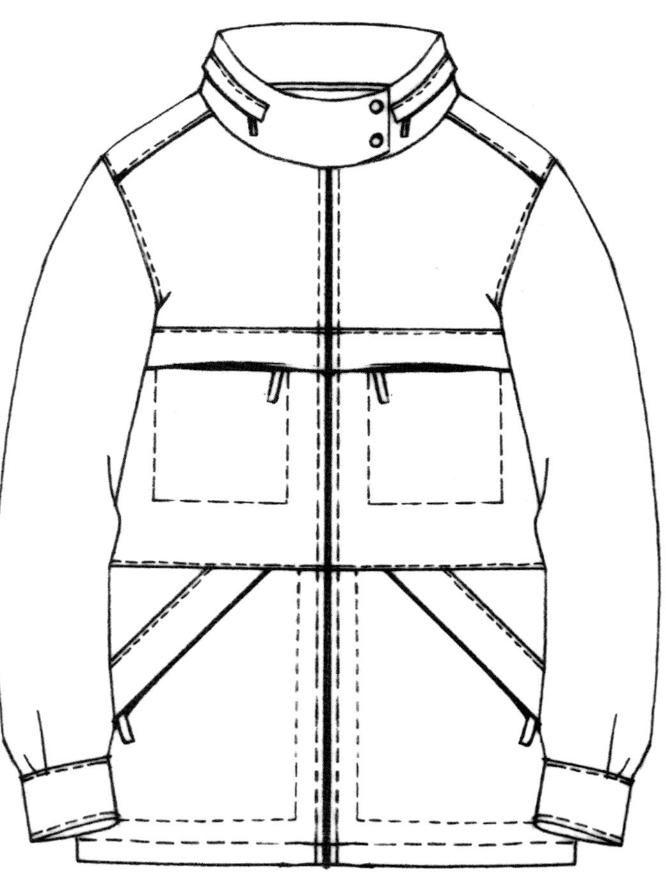
Training parka

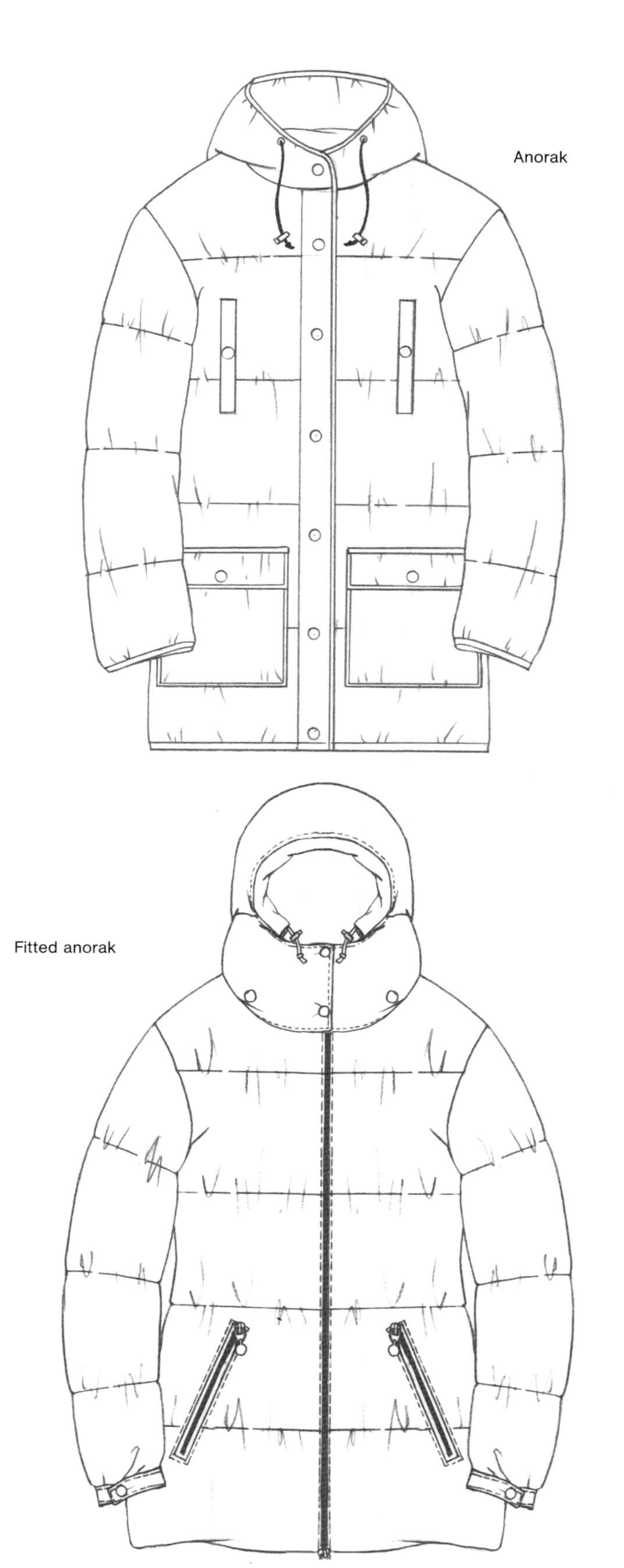
Anorak

Fitted anorak

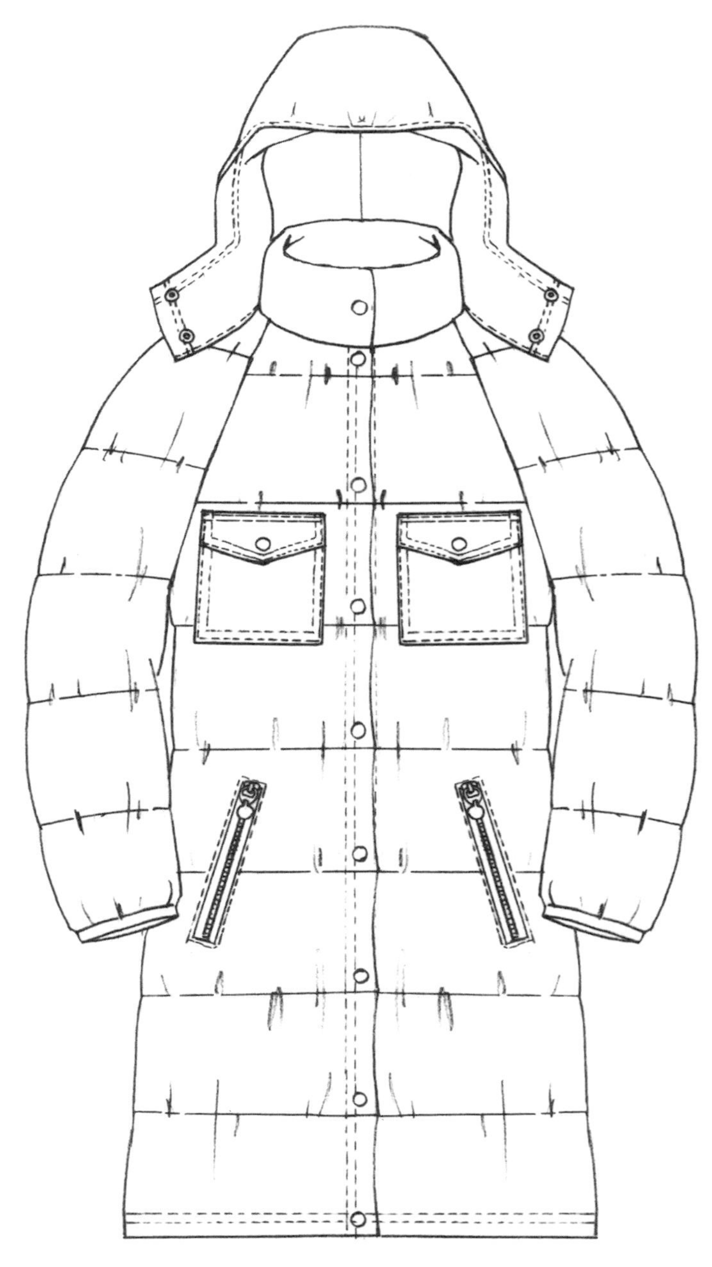
Long anorak / ski jacket

K-Way jacket
Poncho
Anorak raincoat

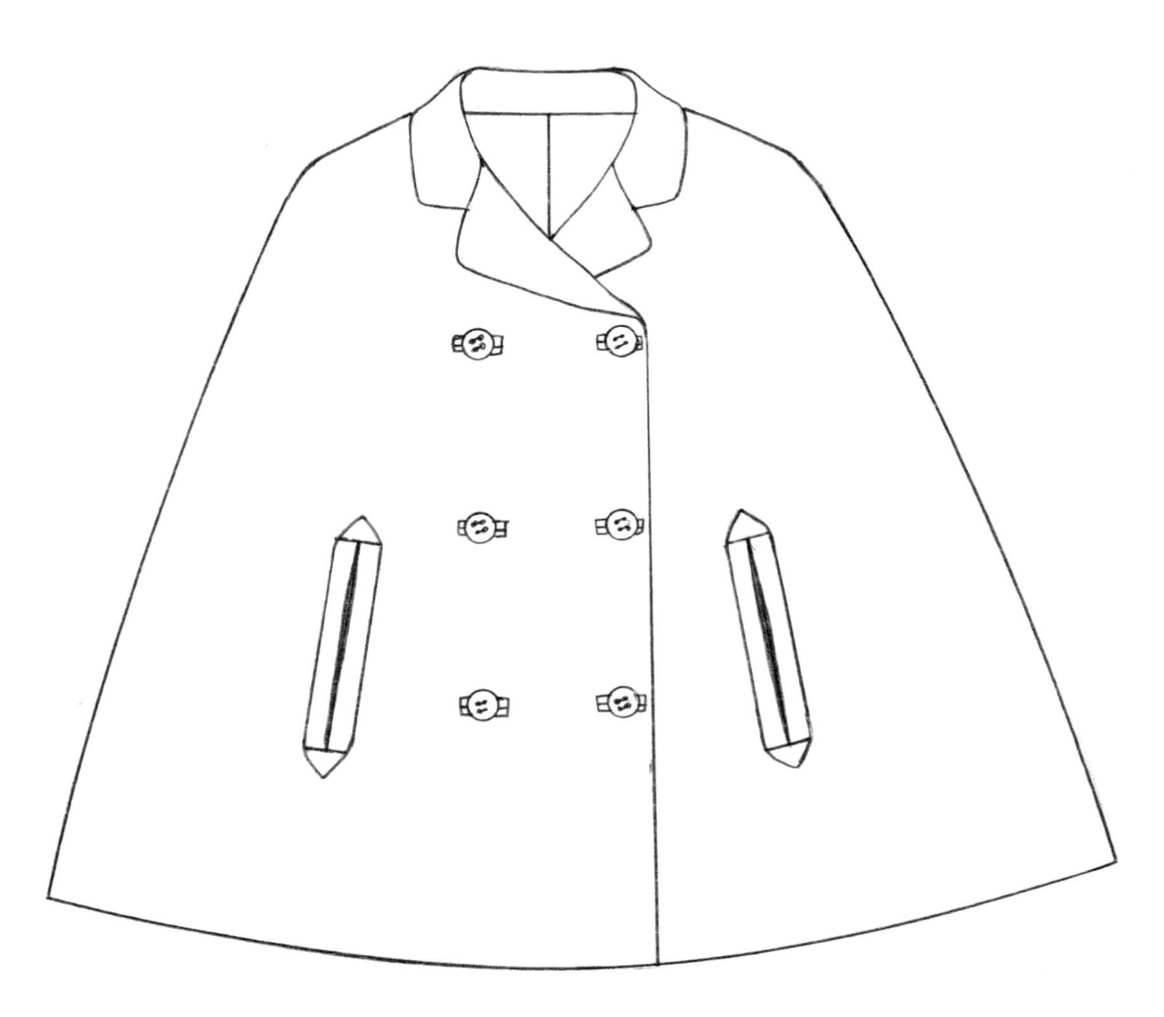

Double-breasted cape

Frock coat, *front*

Frock coat, *profile*

Lingerie
Shoes
& Accessories

Lingerie

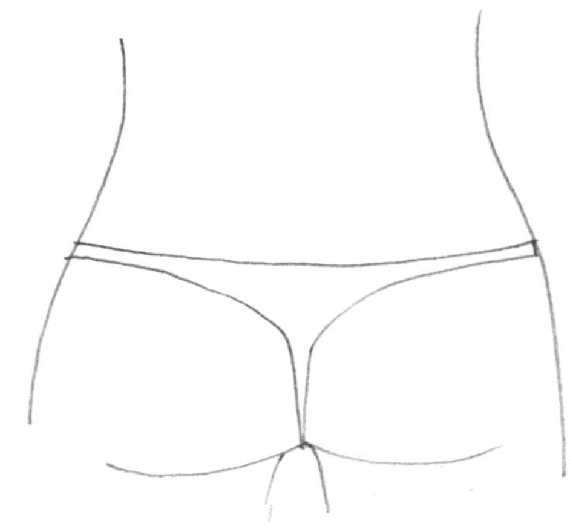

Thong

G-string

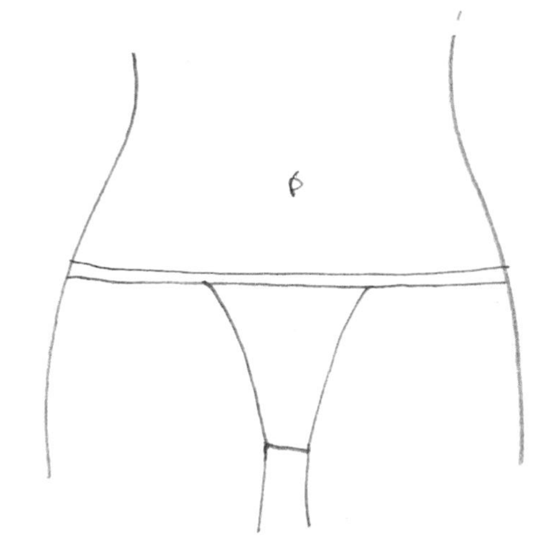

Tanga

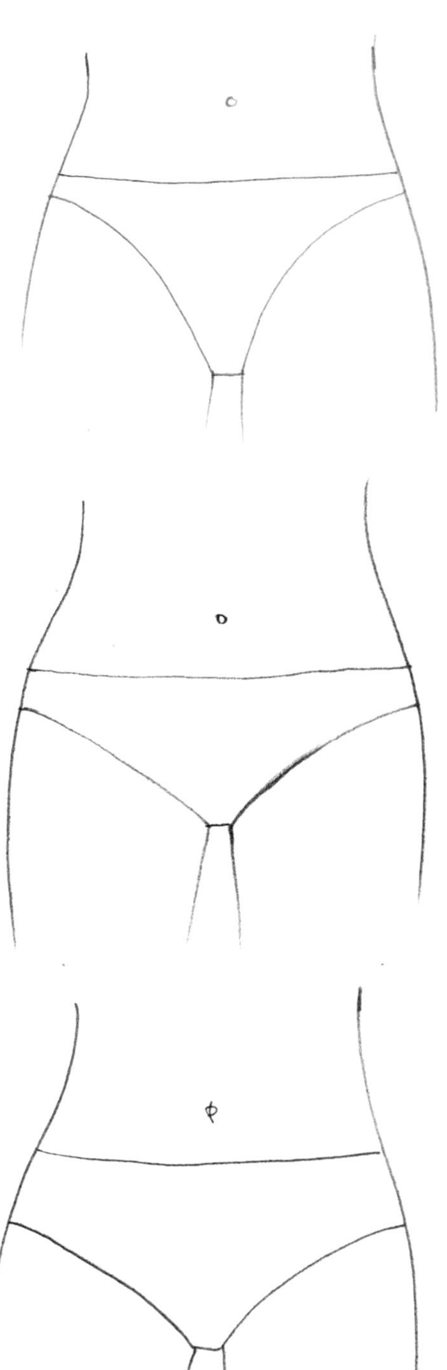

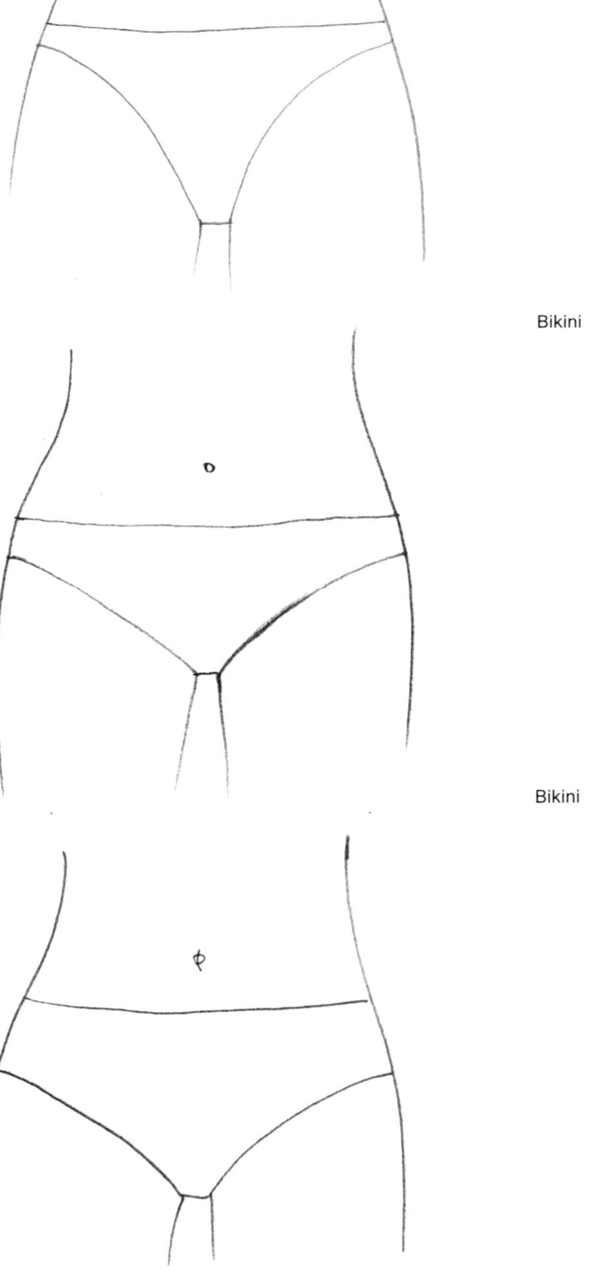

Bikini

Bikini

Briefs

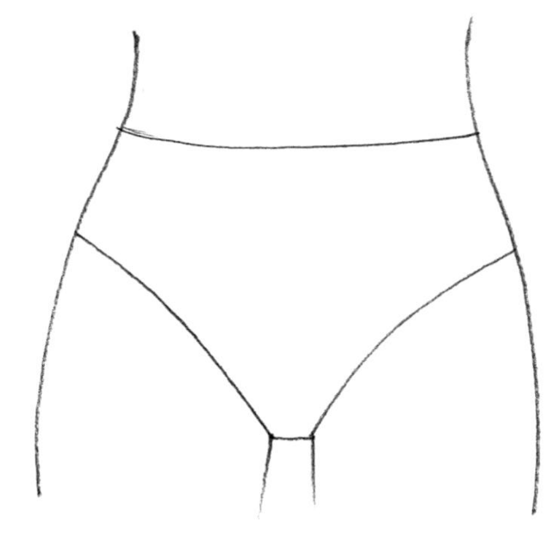

High-waist briefs

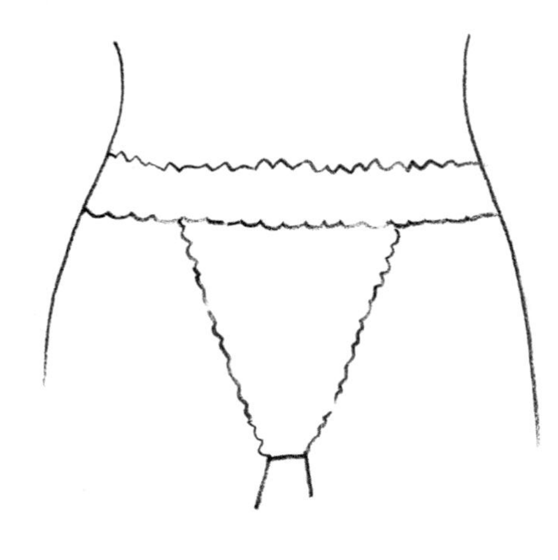

Lace panties

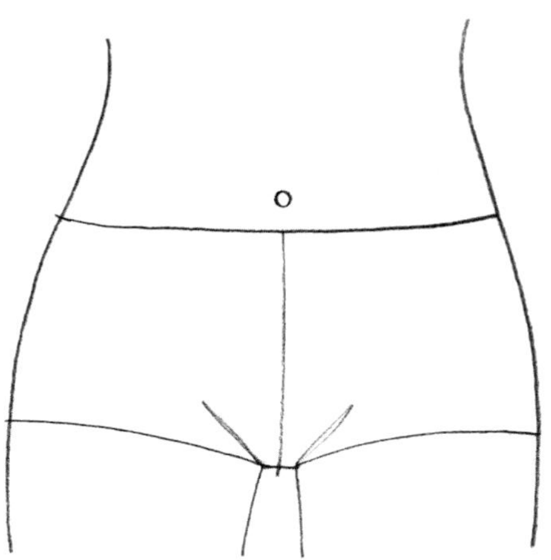

Boy shorts

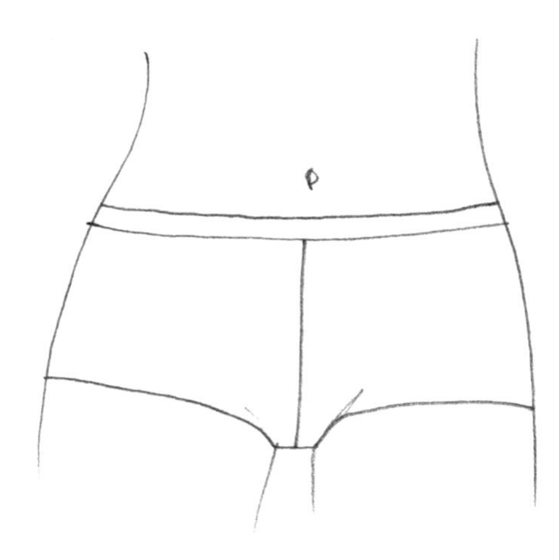

Tanga boy shorts

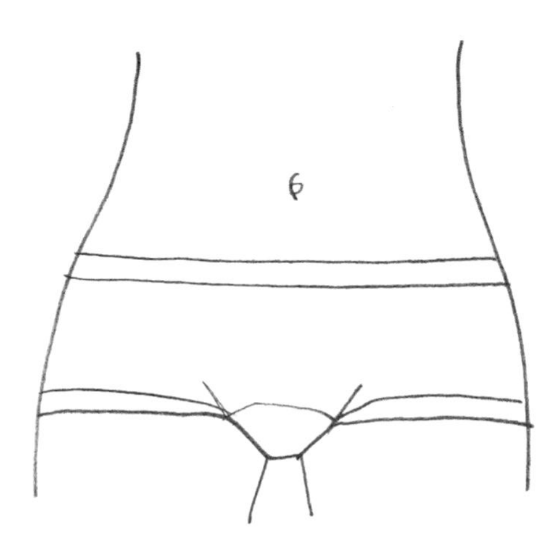

Tube boy shorts

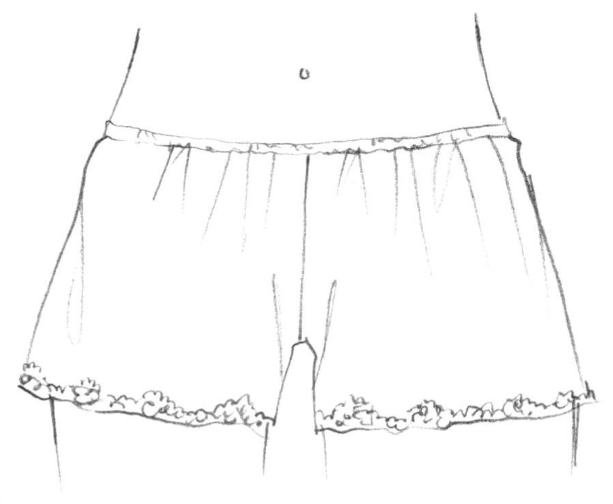

High and low French panties

Décolleté: foam-filled or molded.

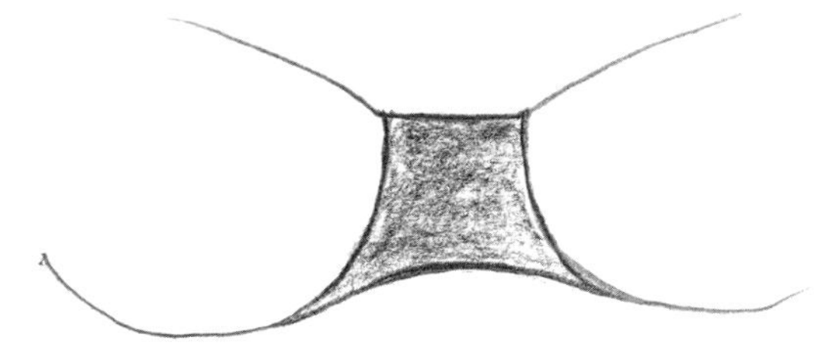

Full center gore

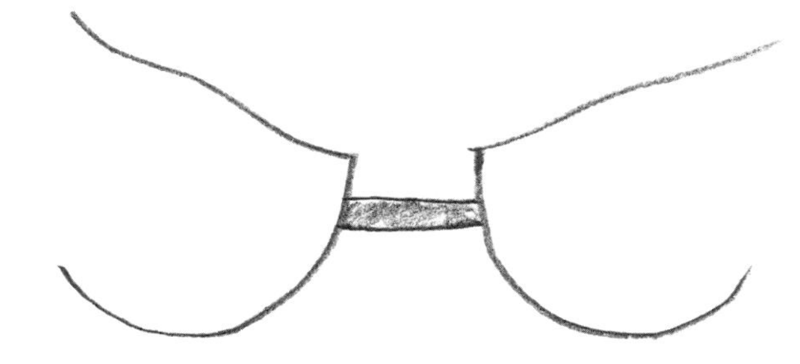

Single-banded center gore

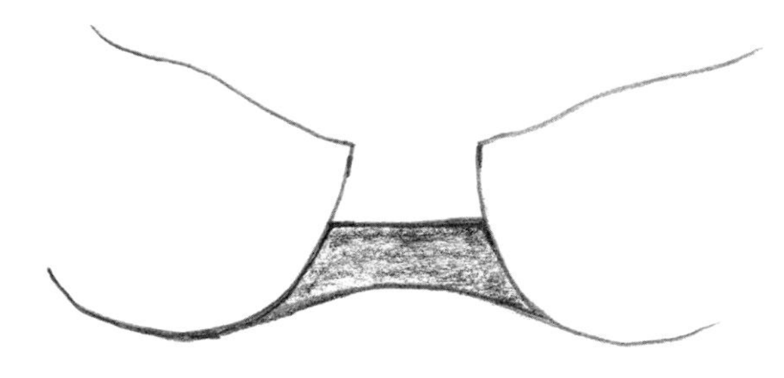

Half center gore

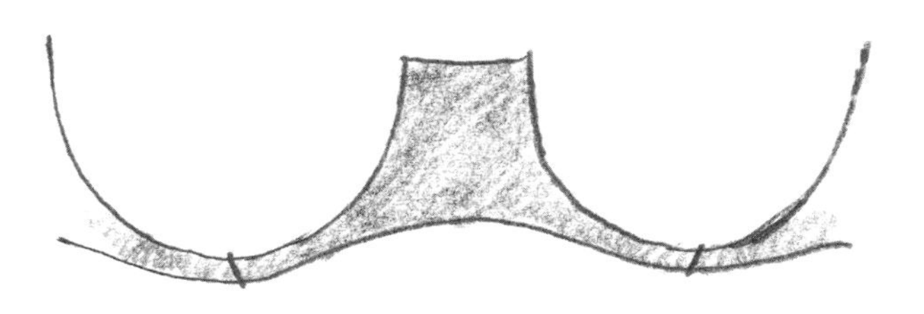

Center gore with inner sling

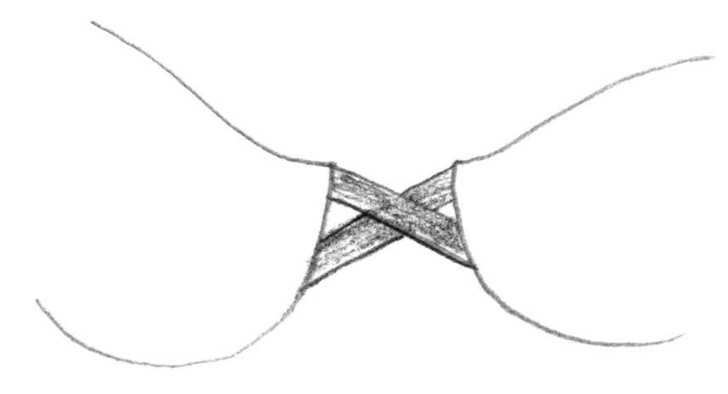

Crossed center gore

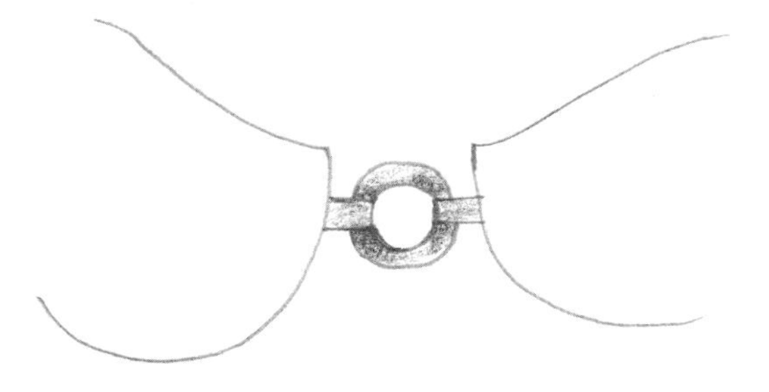

With washer

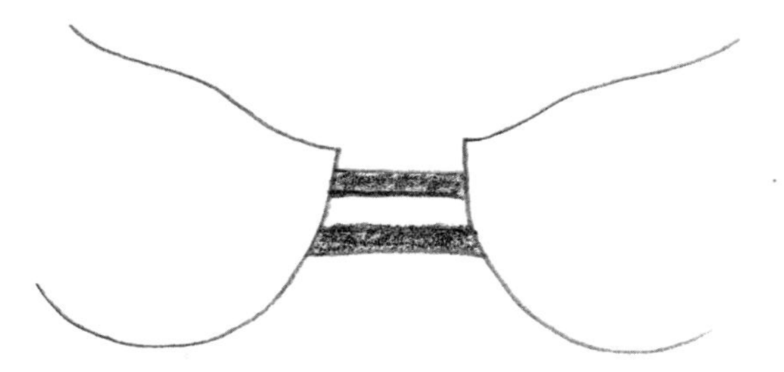

Double-banded center gore

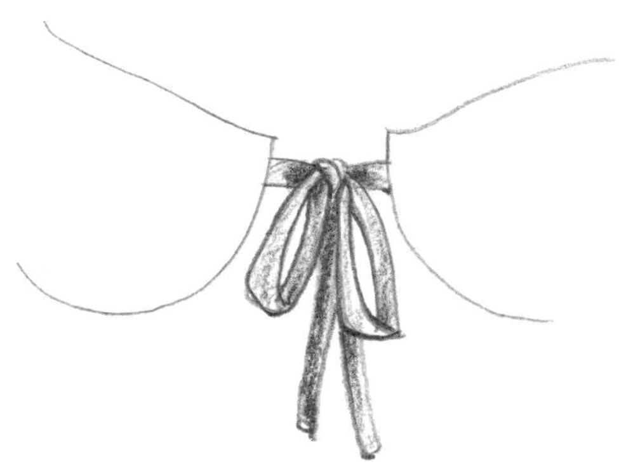

With bow

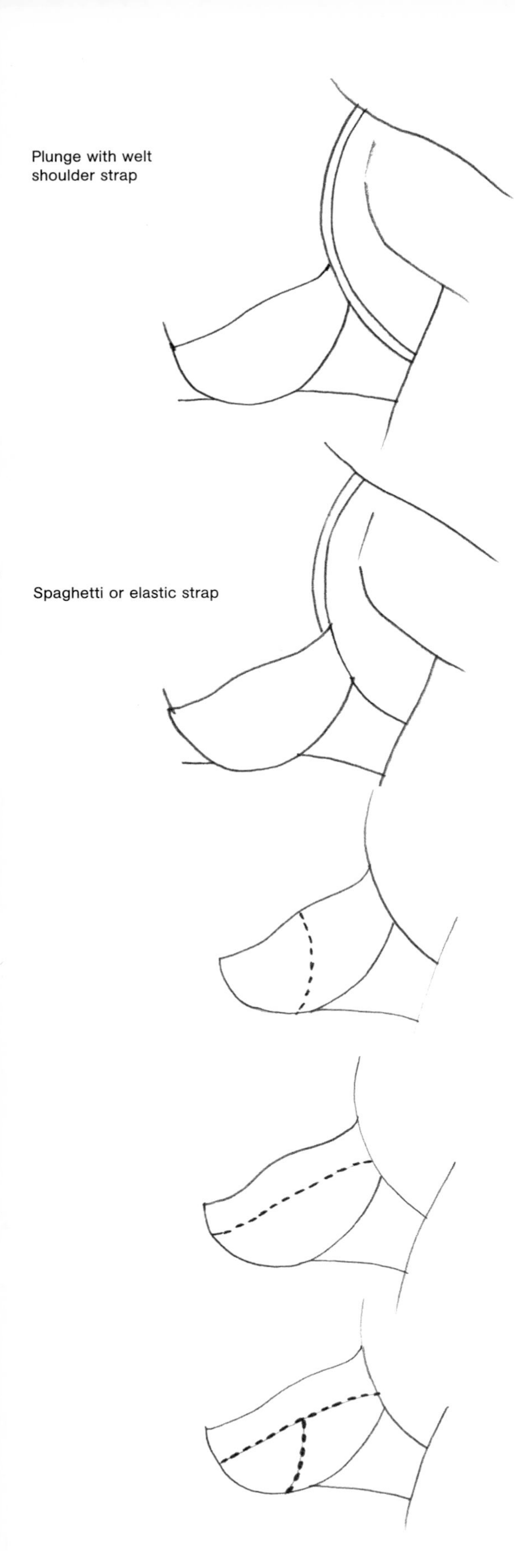
Plunge with welt shoulder strap
Spaghetti or elastic strap

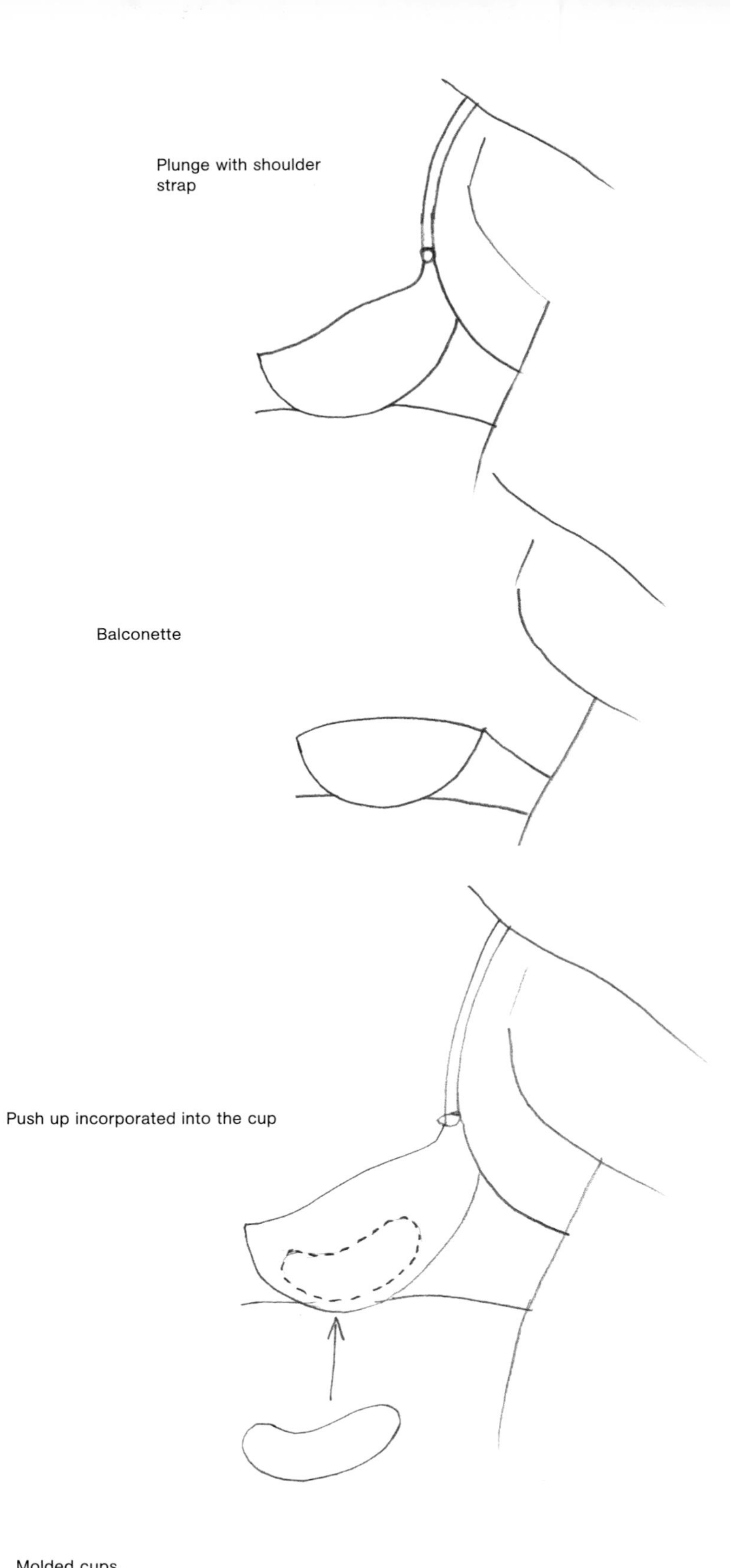
Plunge with shoulder strap
Balconette
Push up incorporated into the cup
Molded cups

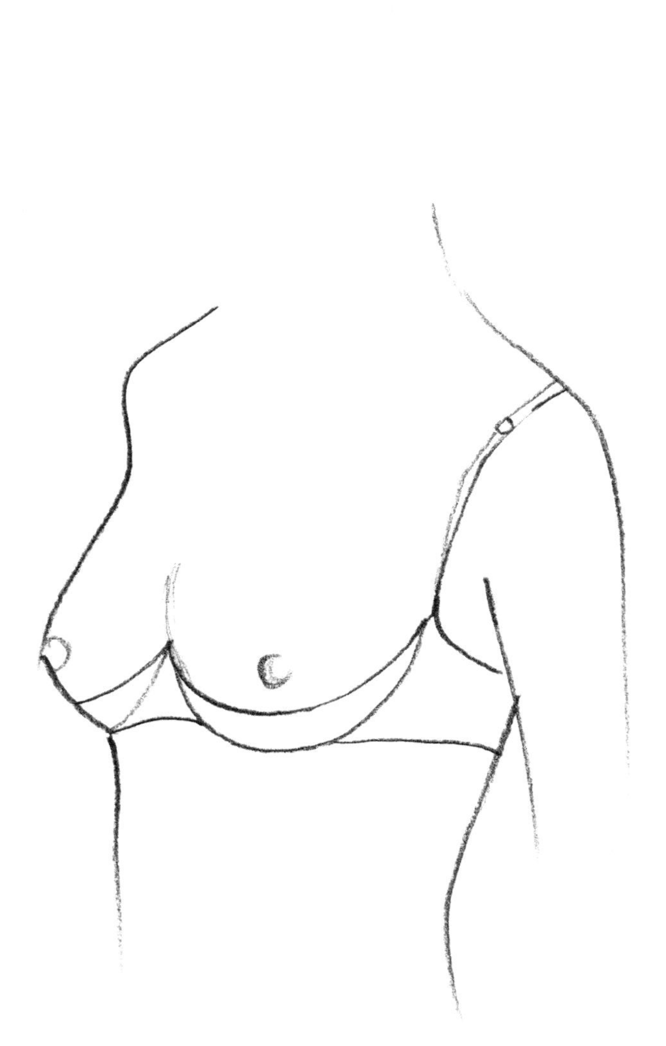

Center gore with inner sling

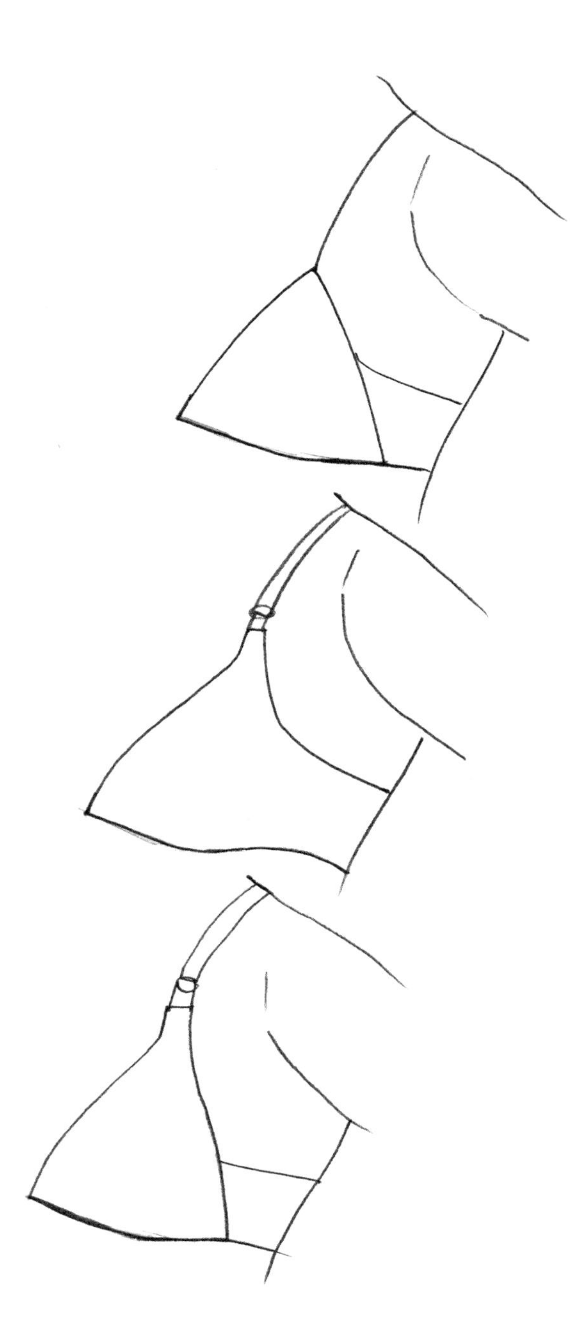

Triangular-shaped cups

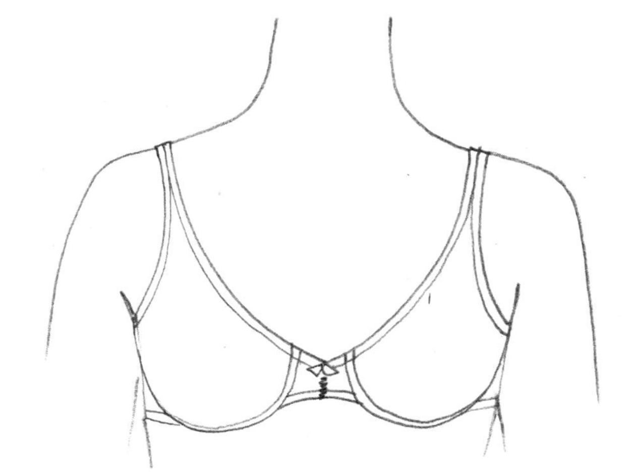

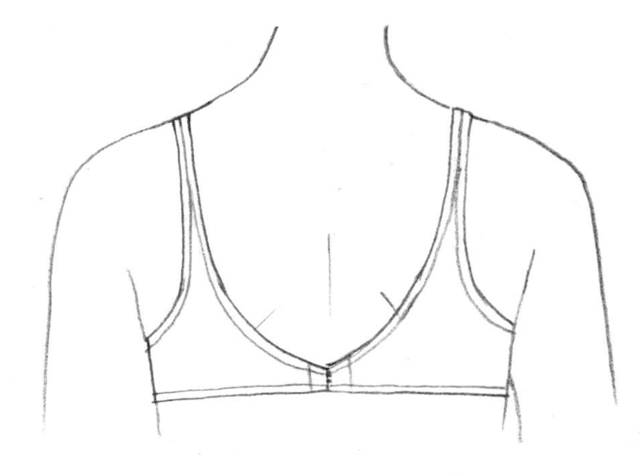

Bra with full center gore

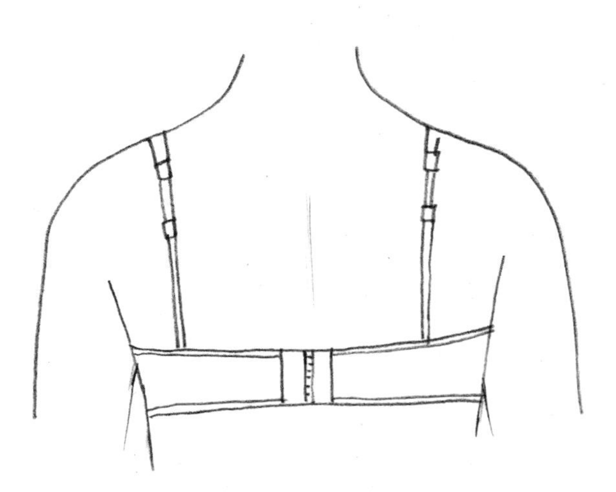

Padded bra

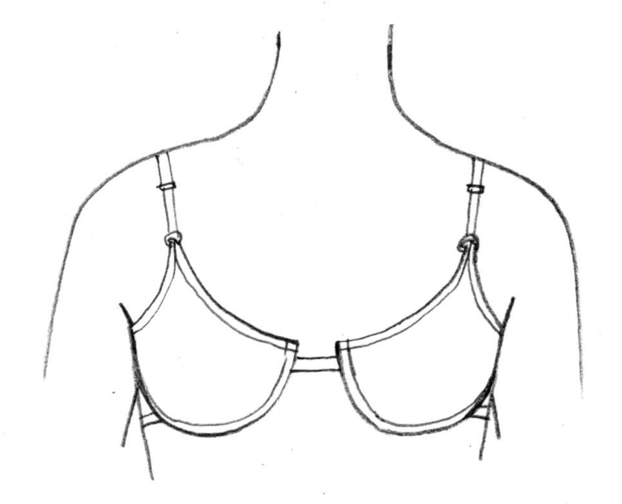

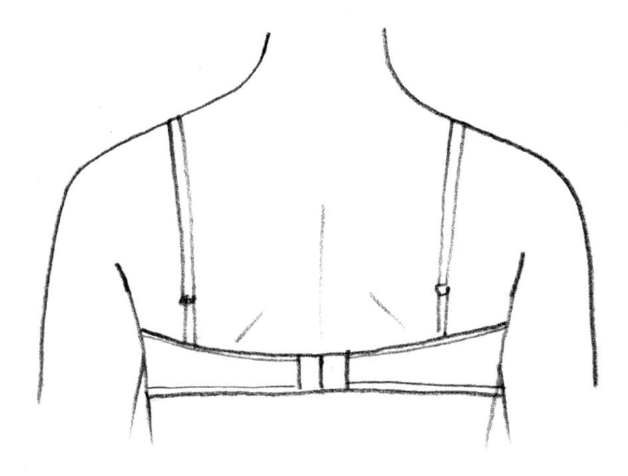

Bra with center gore strap

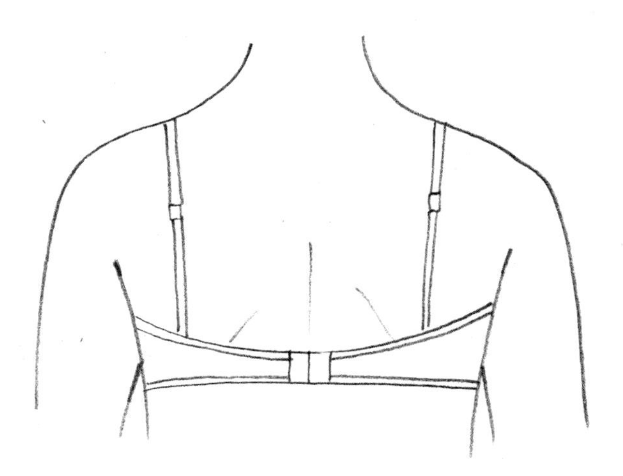

Pleated bra

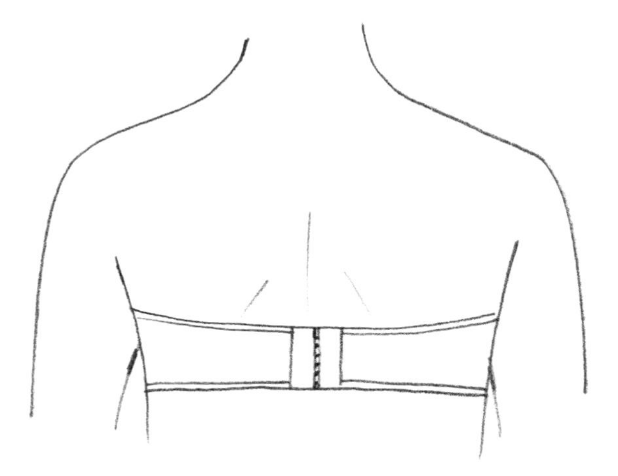

Strapless bra

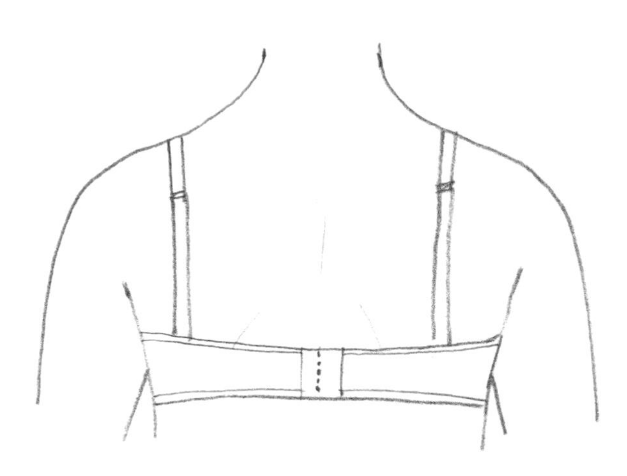

Lace bra

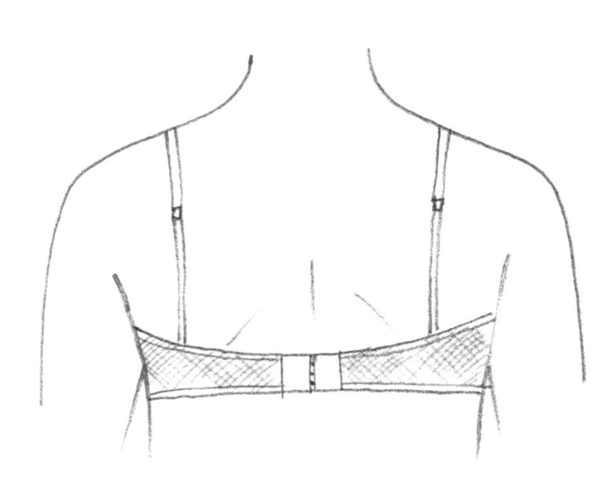

Transparent bra

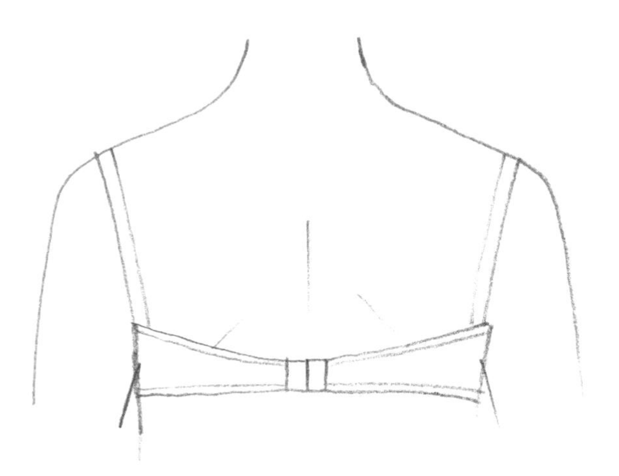

Cotton embroidery bra

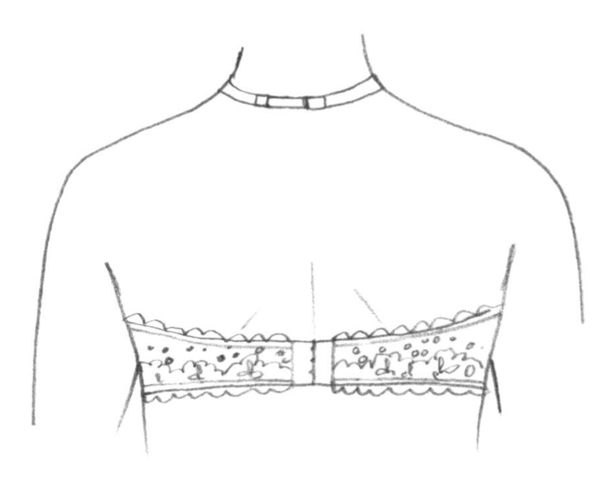

Halter neck bra

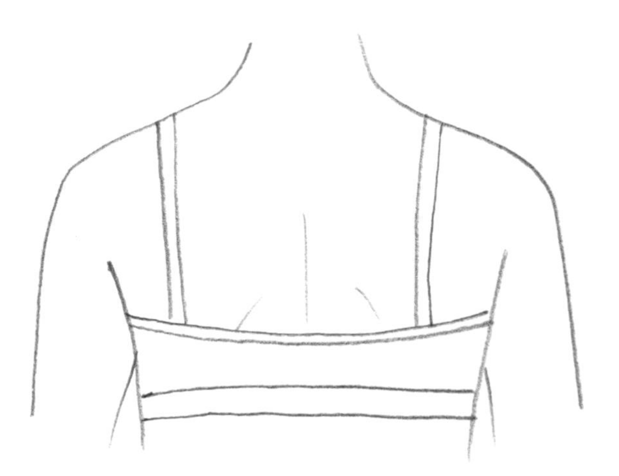

Tube top

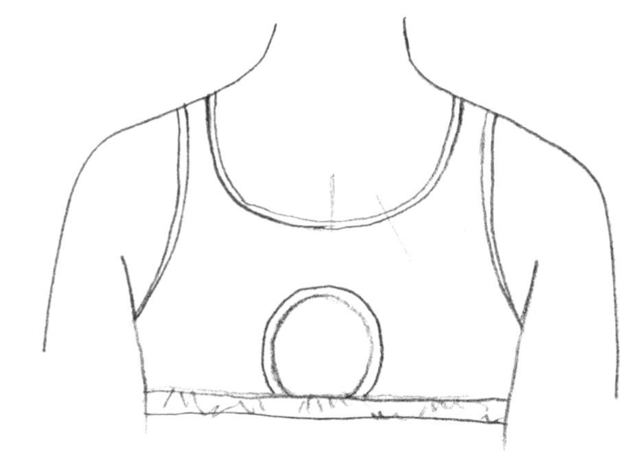

Sports bra

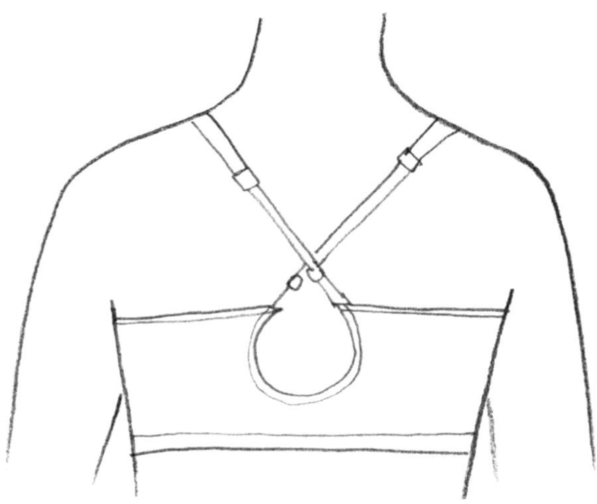

Sports bra, *backs*

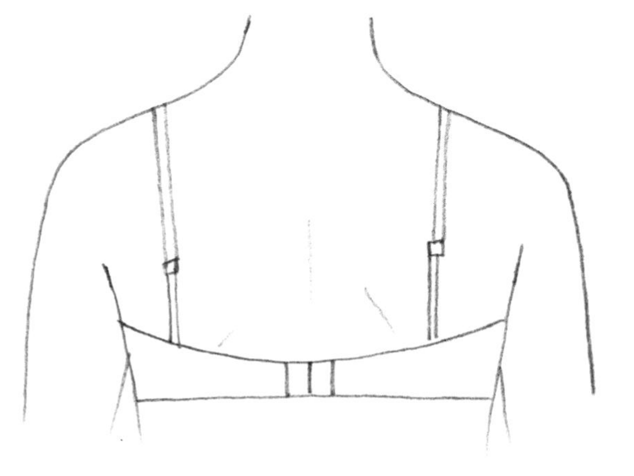

Triangular-shaped bra

Bra top

Lace and satin bodice

Transparent lace bodice

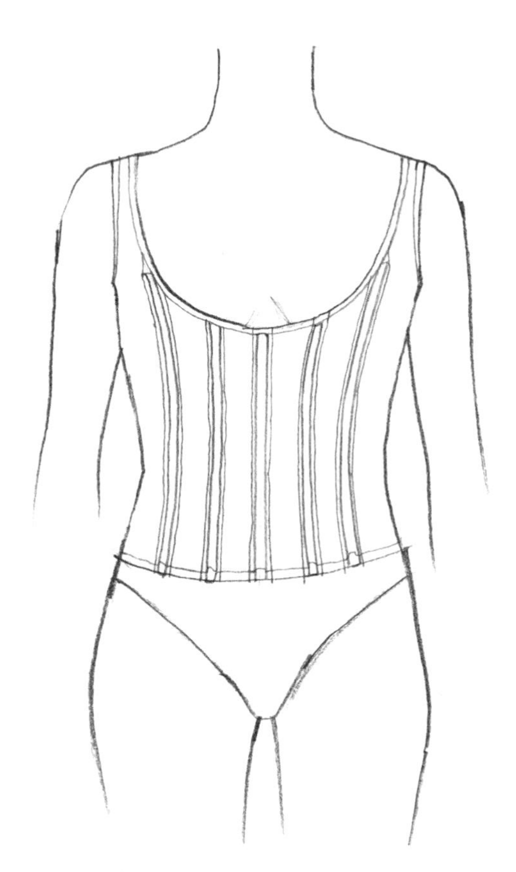

Bodice with rounded neckline

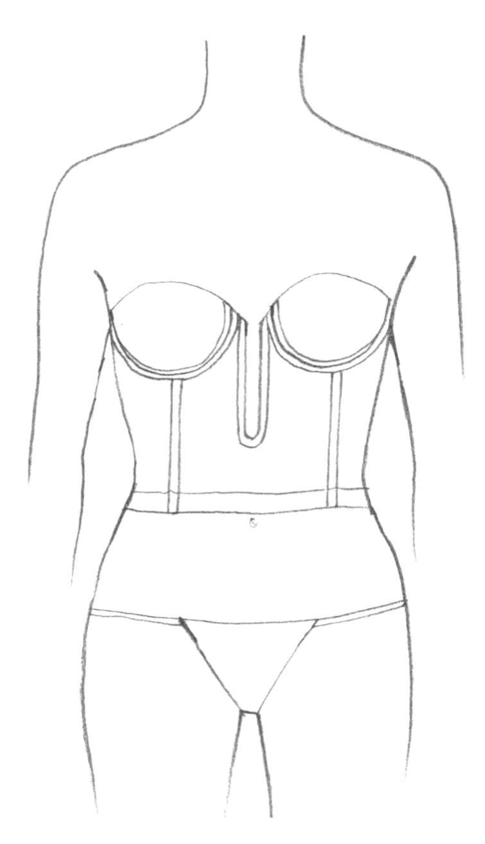

Strapless waist bodice

Bodice with crossed laces

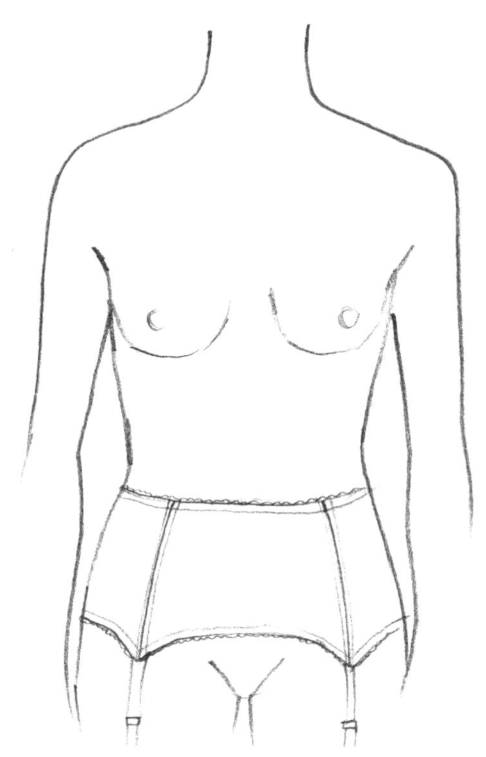

Garter belt

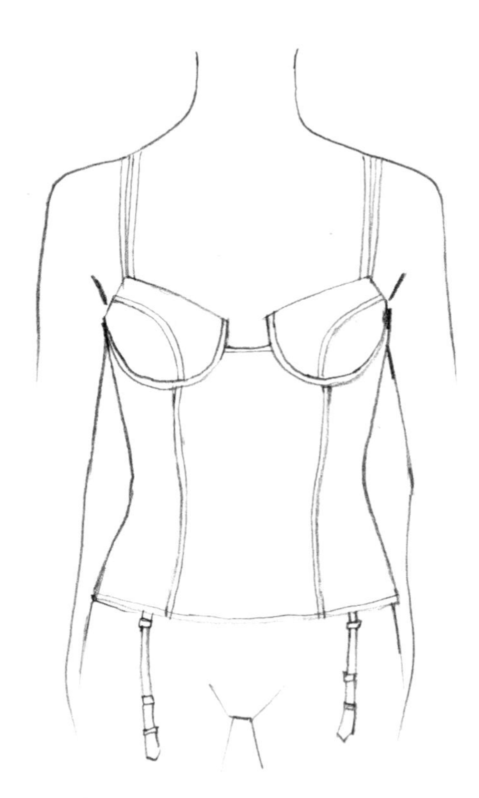

Bodice with garter belt

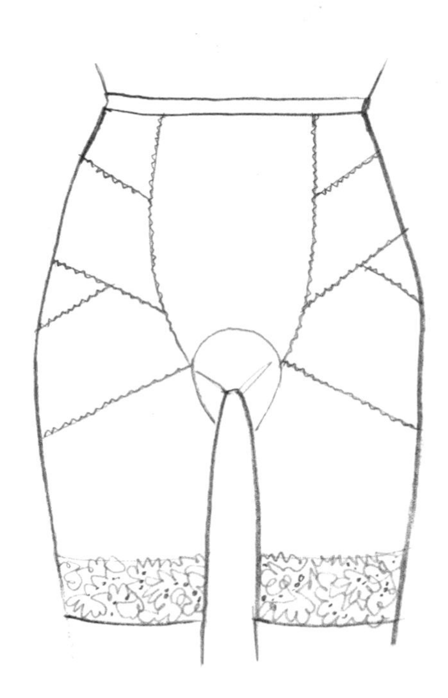

Half-leg girdle

Ensemble of silk lace and tulle

Ensemble of silk lace

Ensemble of superimposed pieces

Ensemble of tulle frills

Lace deco ensemble

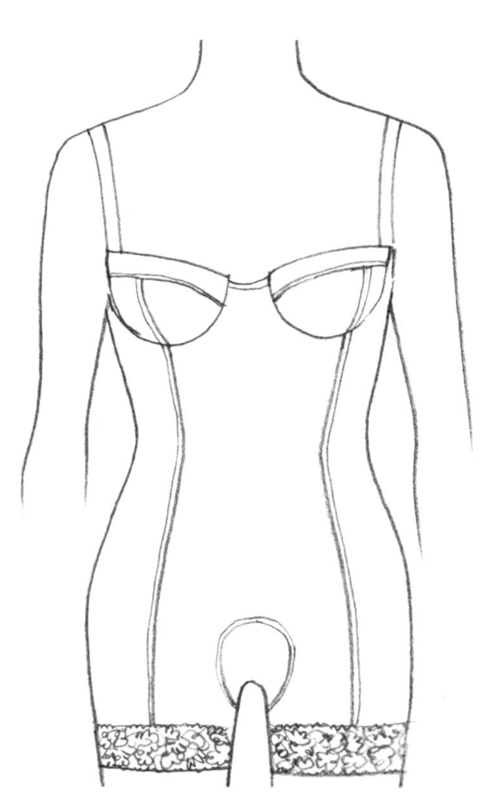

Whole-body girdle

Tops

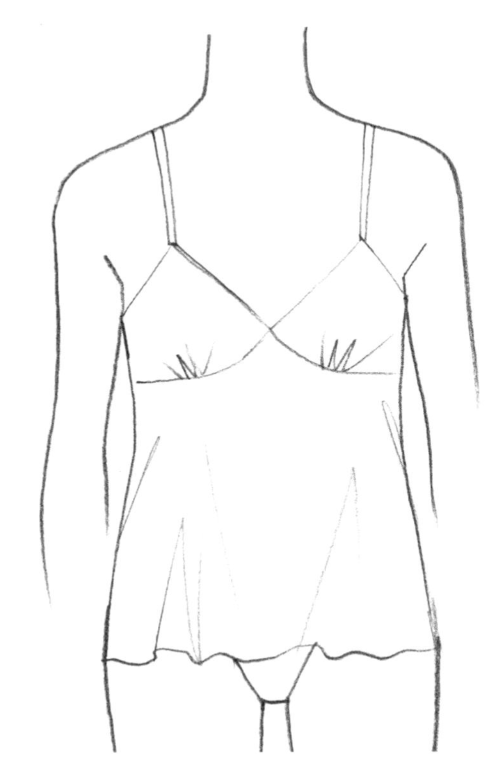

Gathered top

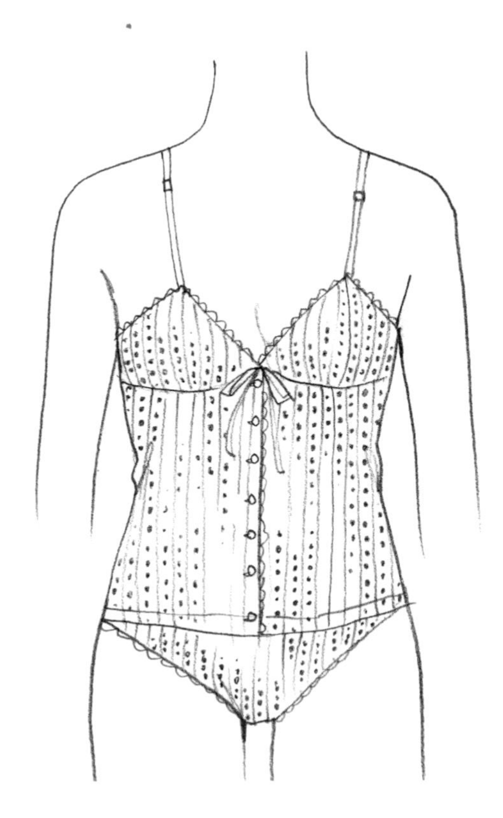

Cotton openwork top

Satin nightgown with 1920s-style lace

Top with slits

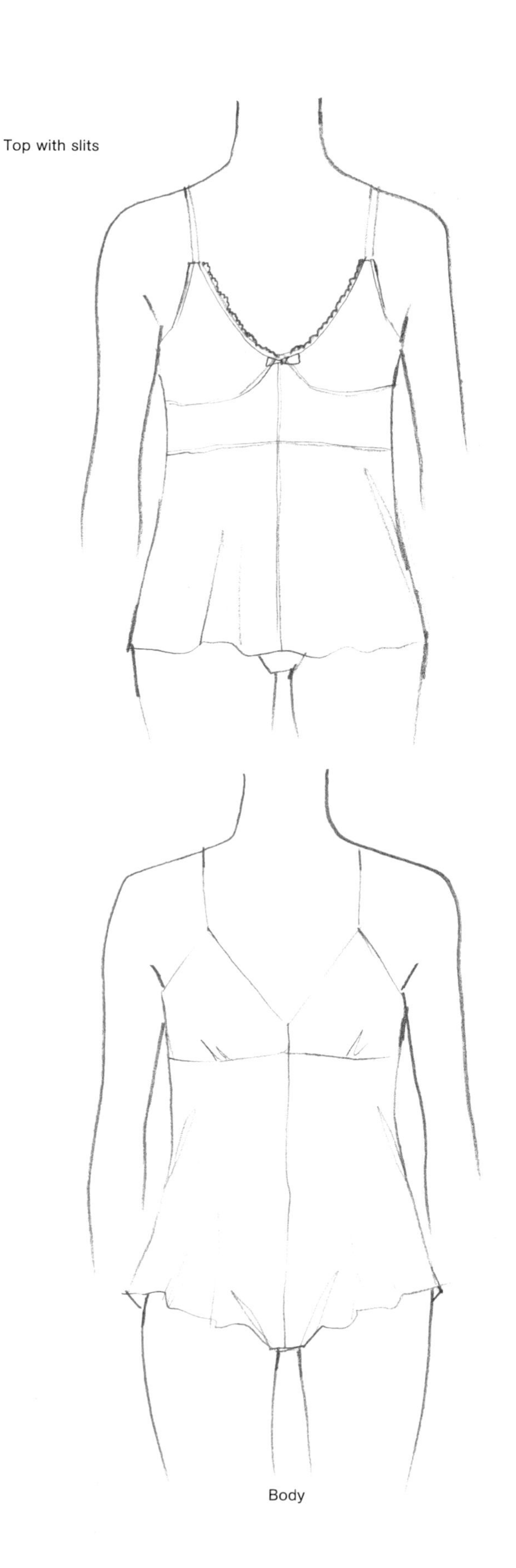

Body

Short 1960s retro nightgown

Transparent ensemble

Romantic cotton nightgown

Classic pajamas

Hooded bath robe

Hooded bathrobe with wide sleeves

Shoes

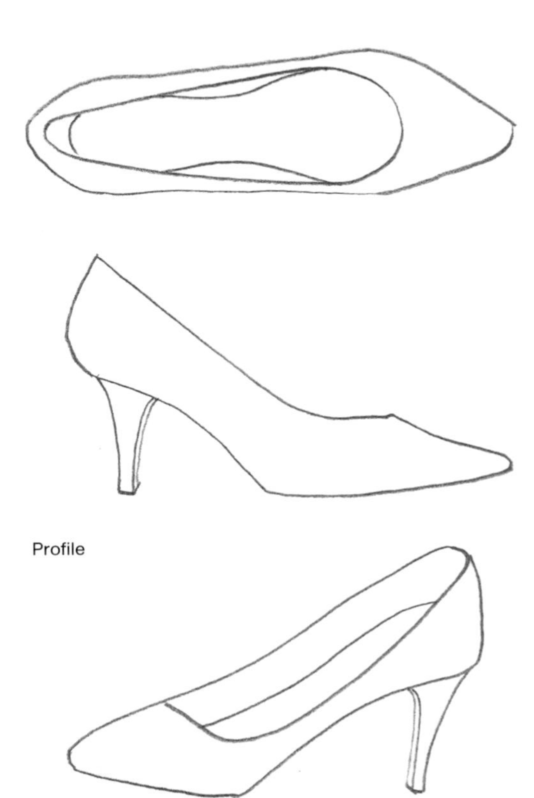

Multiple views of classic pump

Pump

Two-colored slingbacks

Platforms

1970s high heel

Open sides. Jewel ornament

Beaded sandal

Retro perforated pump

With sequins and netted flower

1970s sandal

Evening sandal

Retro, gathered, and with strap

Platform

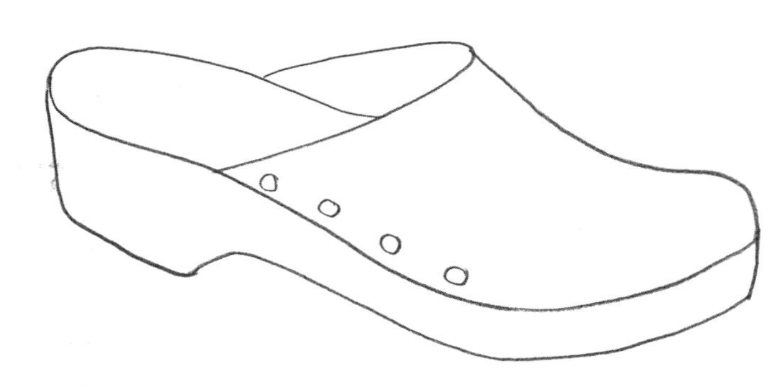

Clog

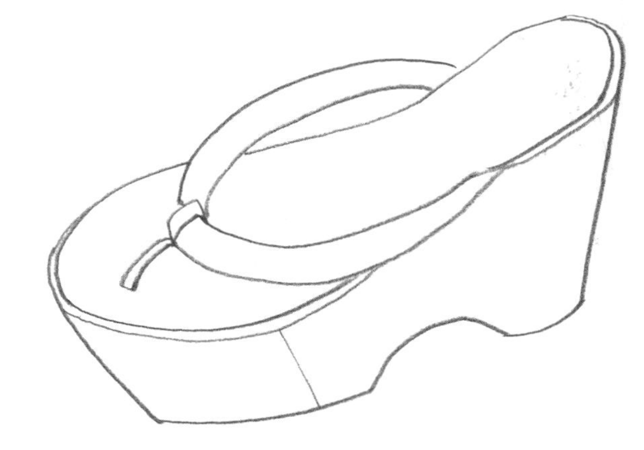

Revived Japanese clog

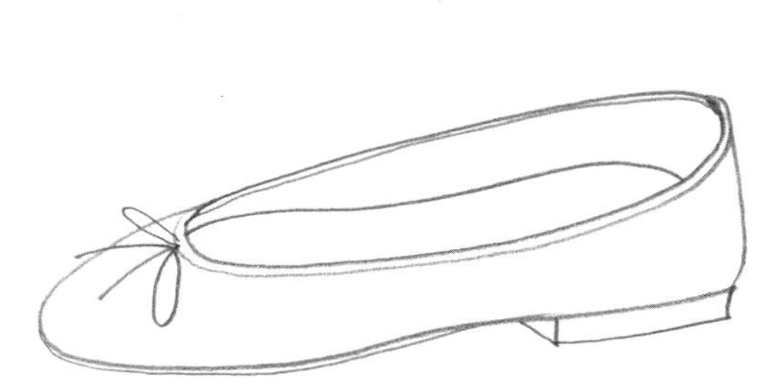

Ballet flats

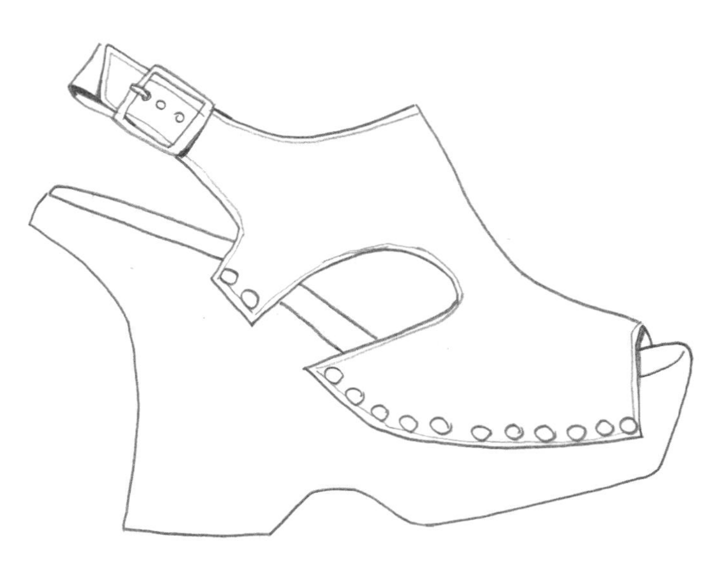

1970s clog

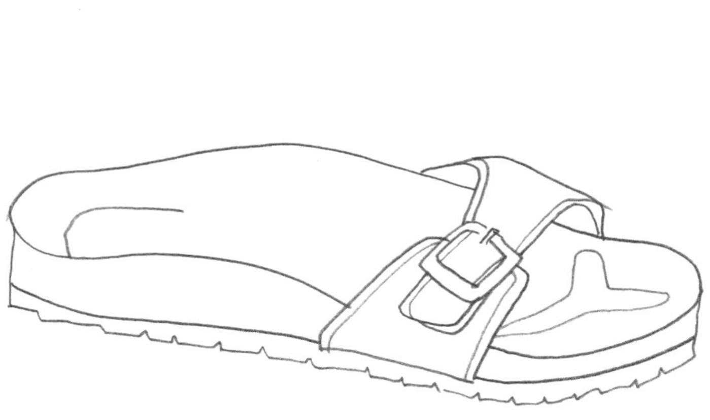

Exercise sandal

Flip-flop

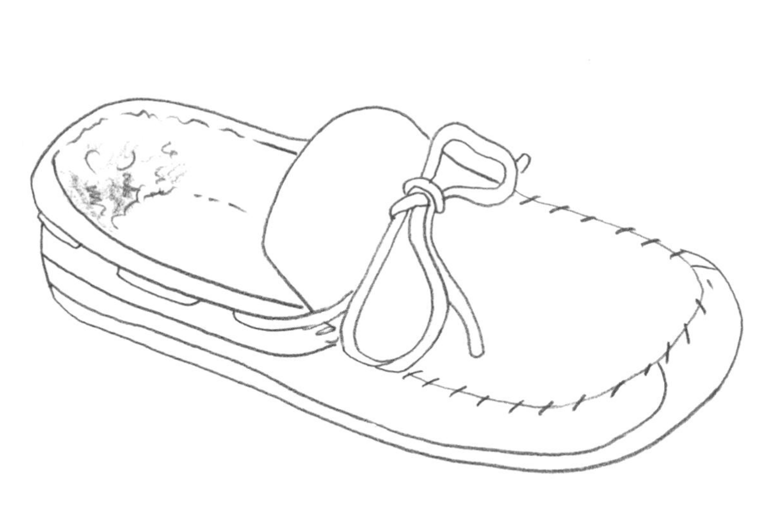

Moccasin

Classic Oxford shoe

Sports shoe with and without Velcro

Sneakers

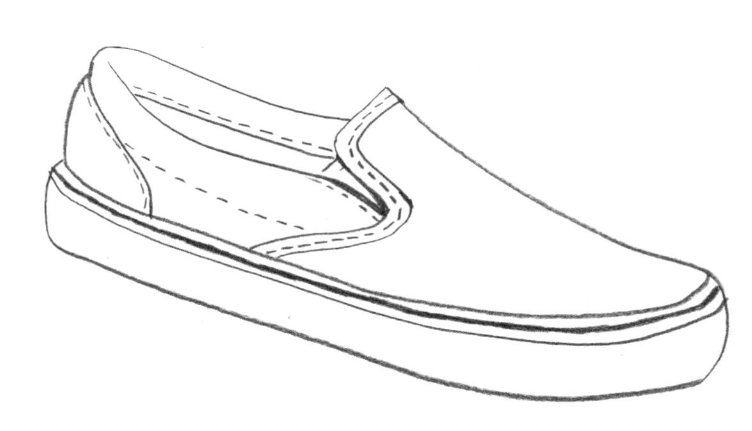

Beach shoe

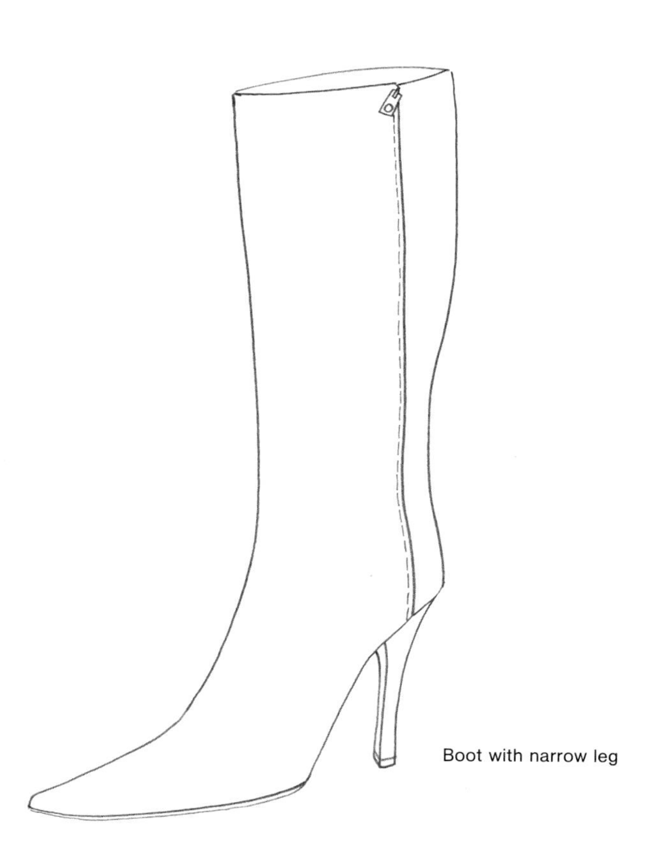

Boot with narrow leg

Boot with fur

Cowboy boot

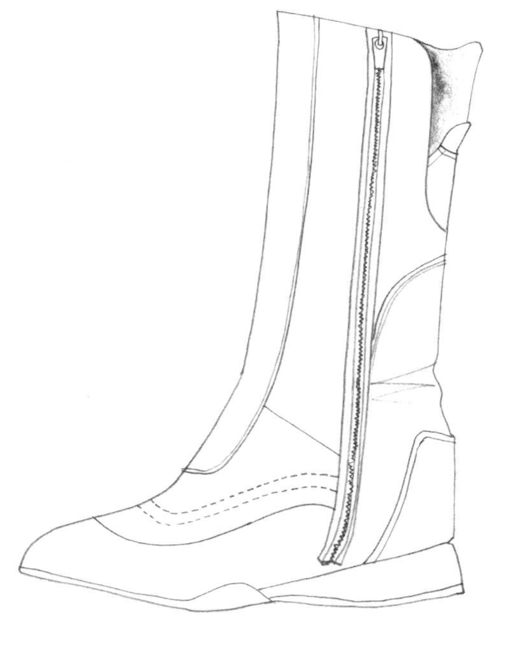

Calf-length boot

Accessories

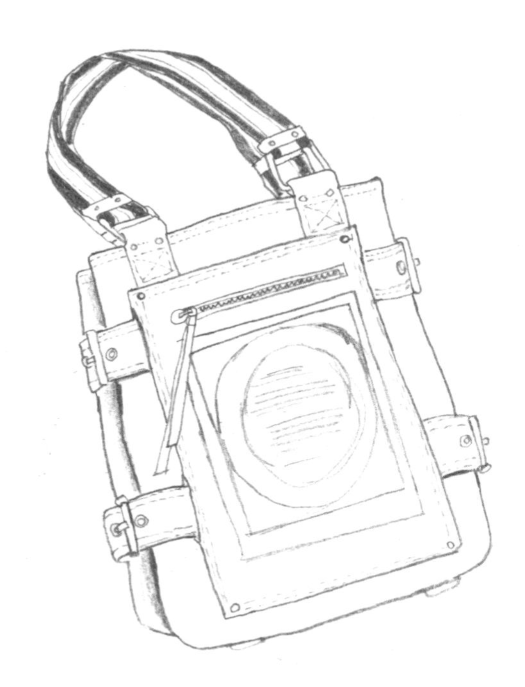

Industrial bag

Small bag with giant buckle

Bag with scarf

Printed

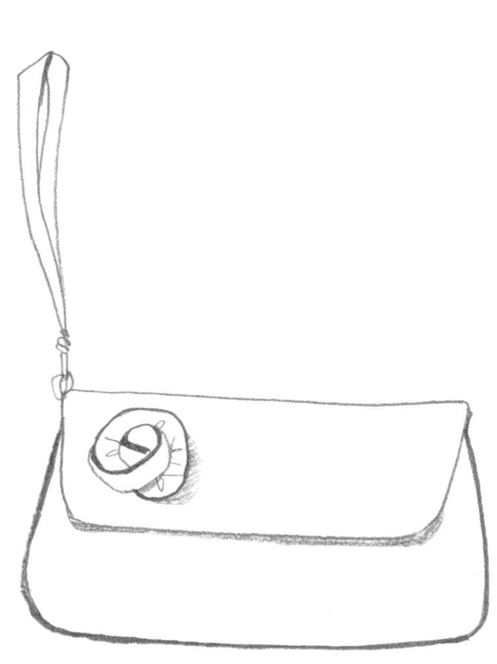
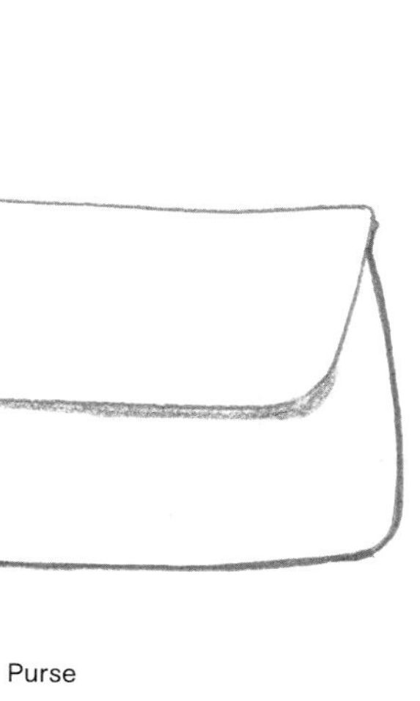

Purse

Bag with leather reinforcement

Bag/briefcase with compartments

Padded bag

Retro

Classic

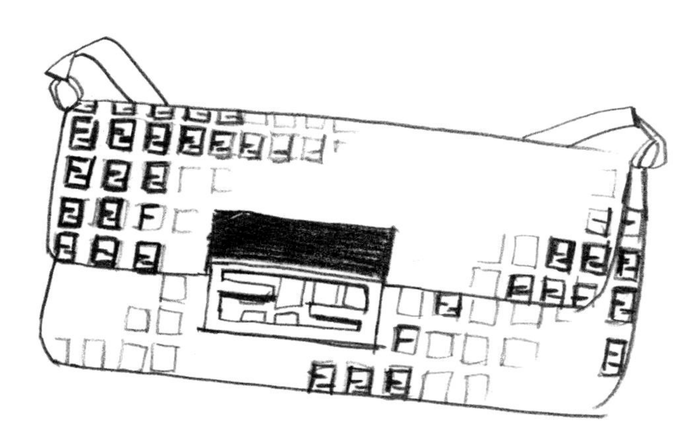

Baguette bag

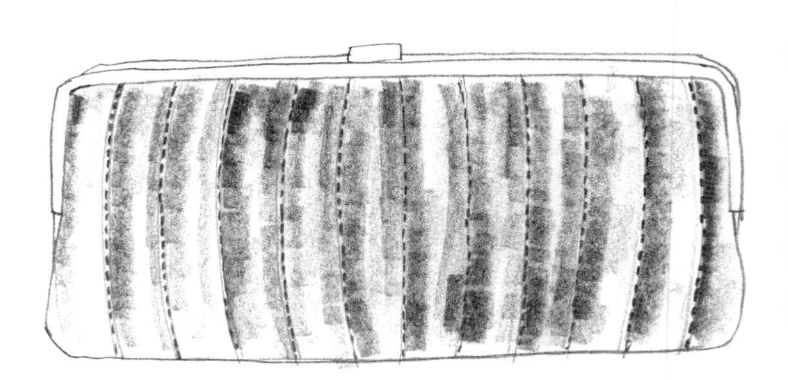

Padded purse

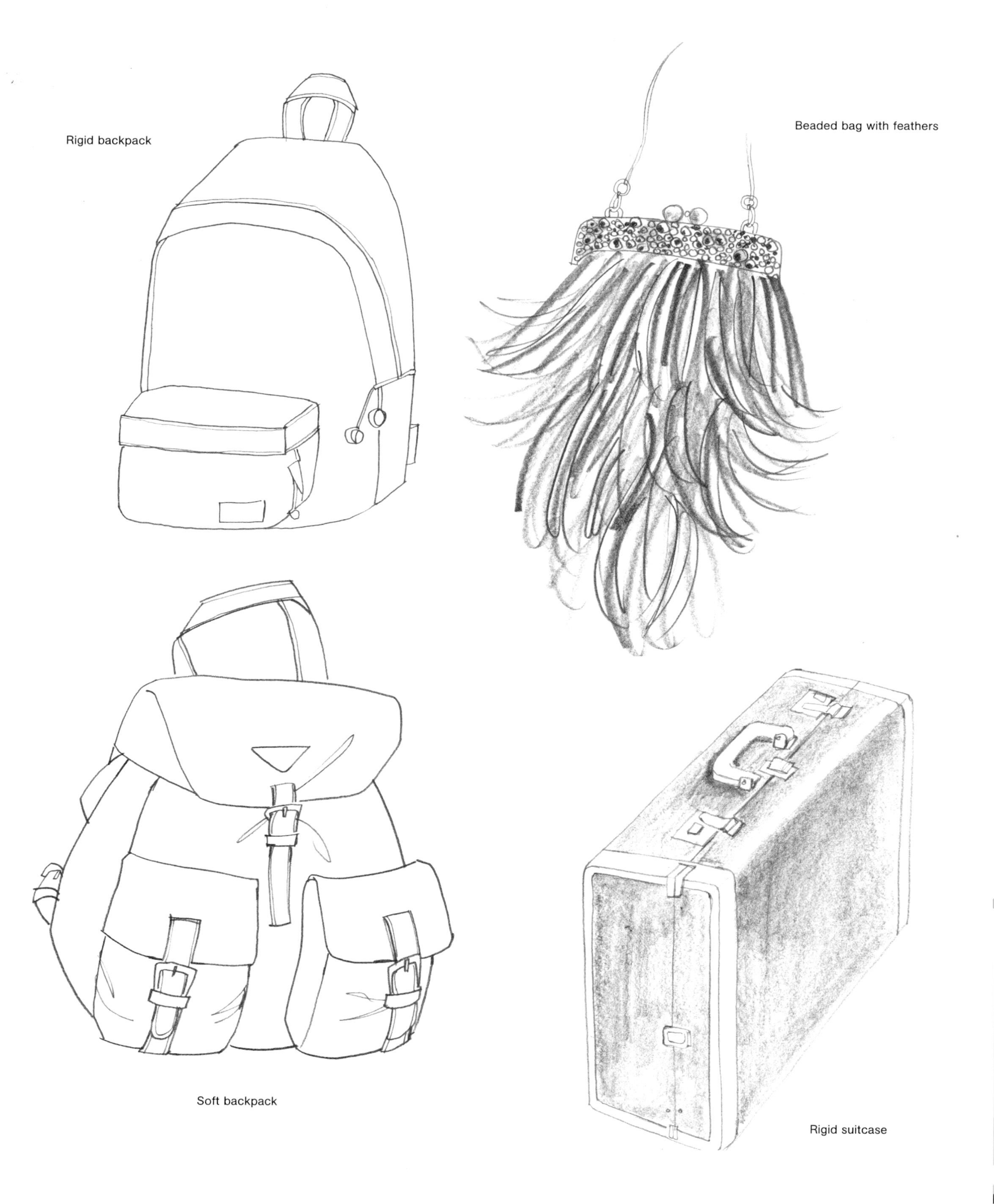
Rigid backpack
Beaded bag with feathers
Soft backpack
Rigid suitcase

Executive laptop bag

Soft laptop case

Multi-zip travel bag

Suitcase with wheels

Laptop briefcase

Bag with front pocket

Sports bag

Knitted bag with rigid handle

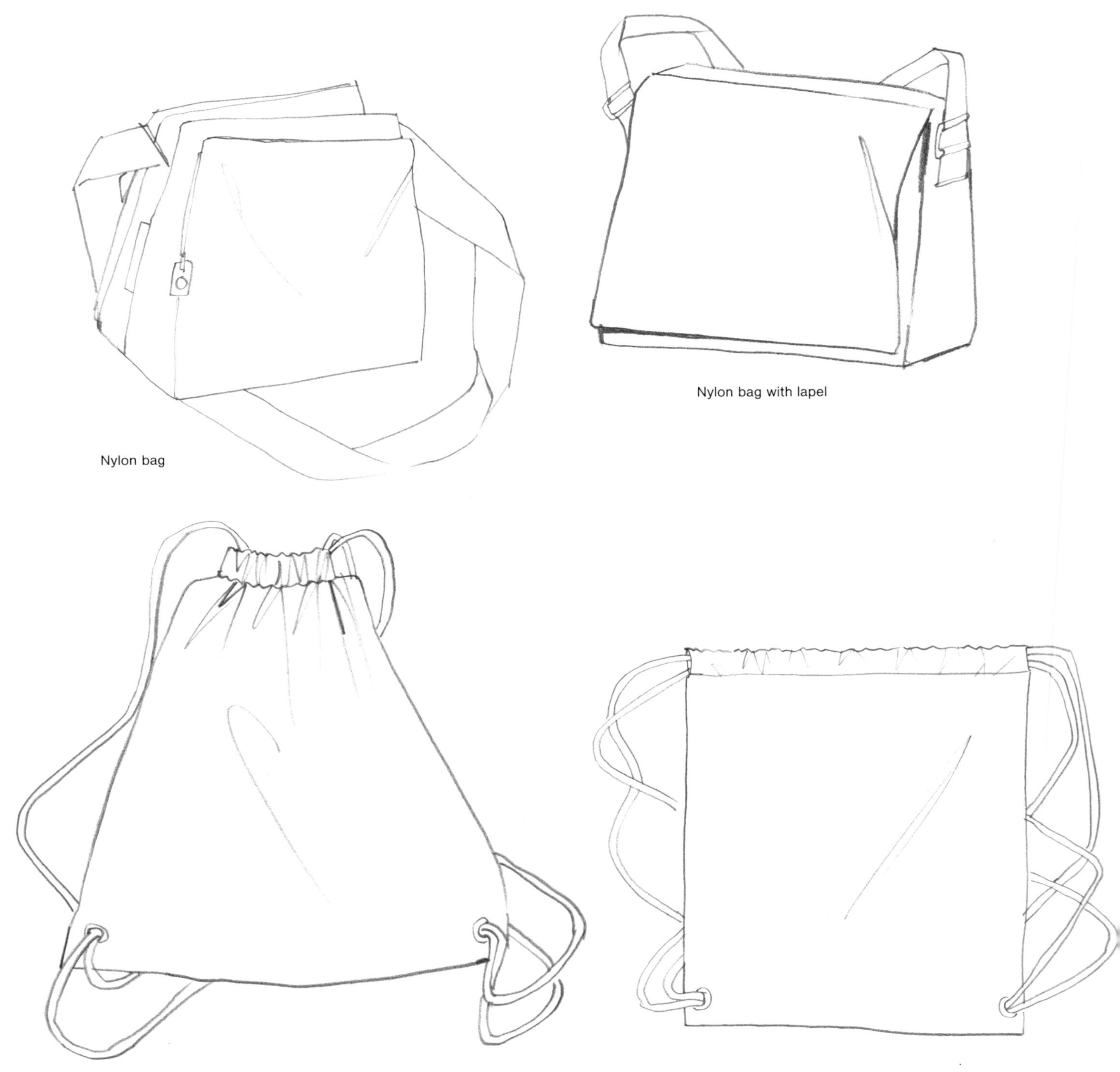

Nylon bag

Nylon bag with lapel

Nylon bag, closed and open

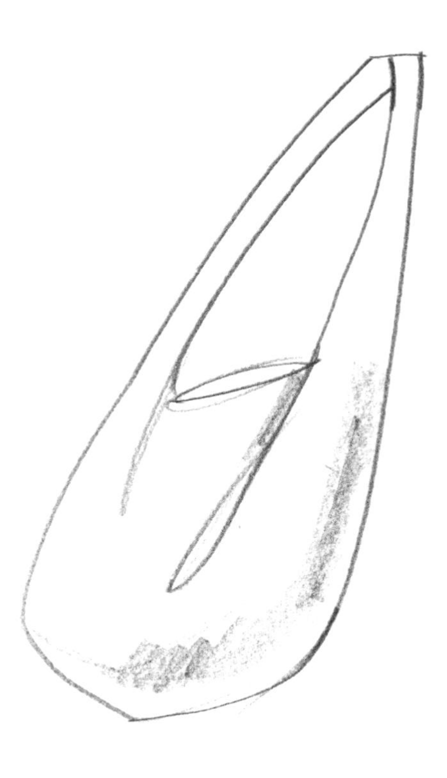

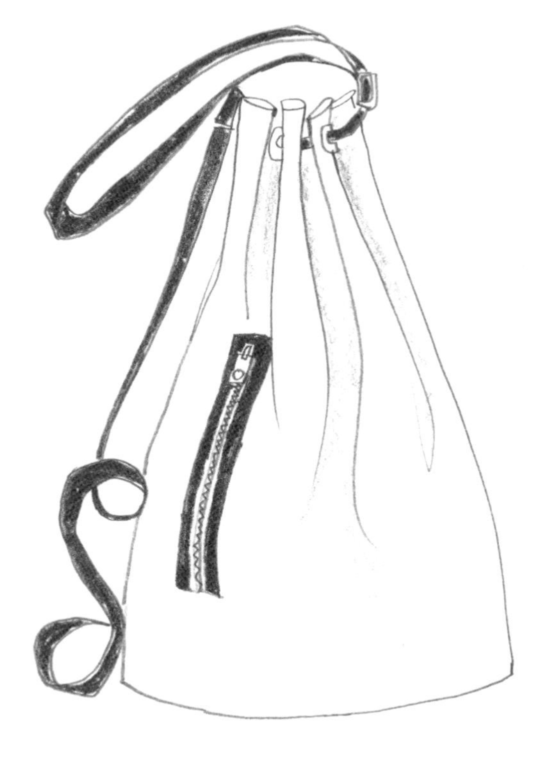

Soft bags

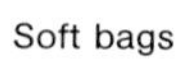

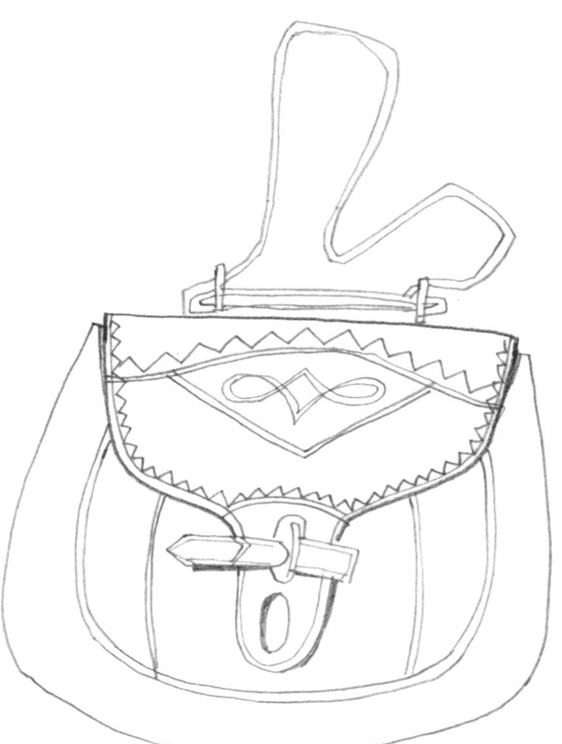

Leather bags

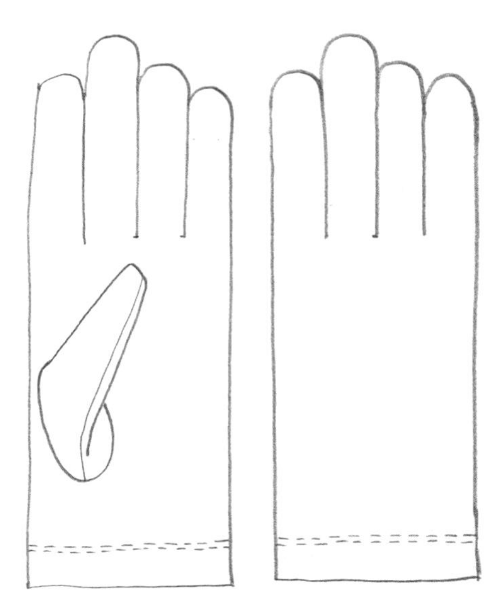

Classic gloves

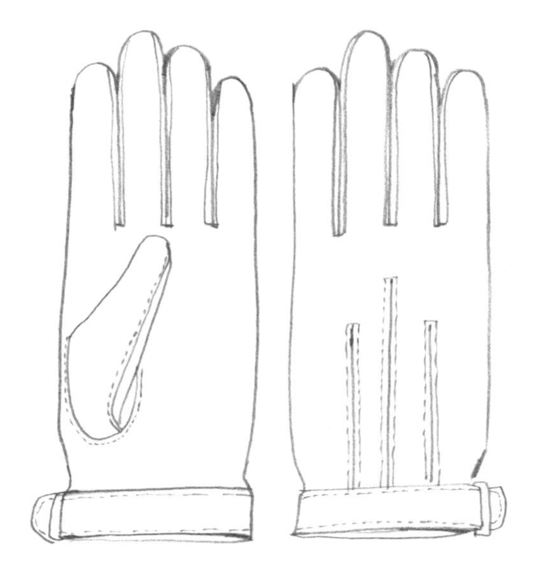

Classic leather gloves

Gloves with perforated Velcro

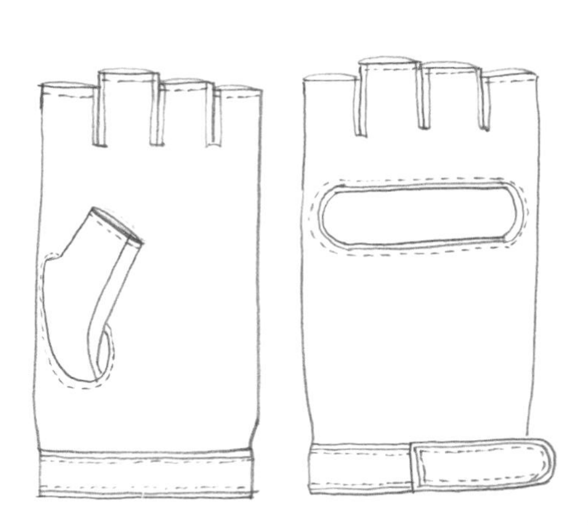

Fingerless Gloves

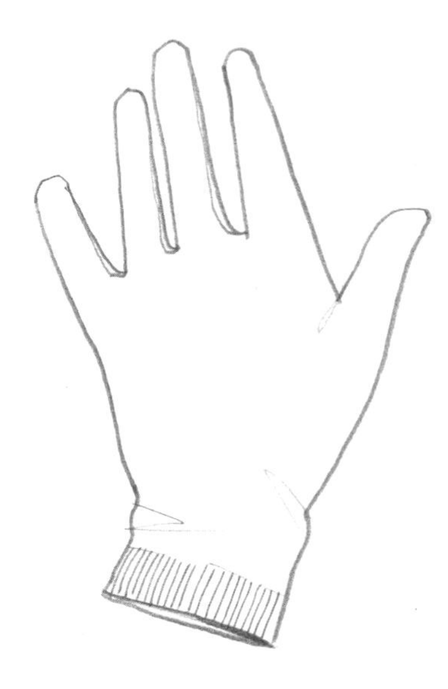
Plain gloves

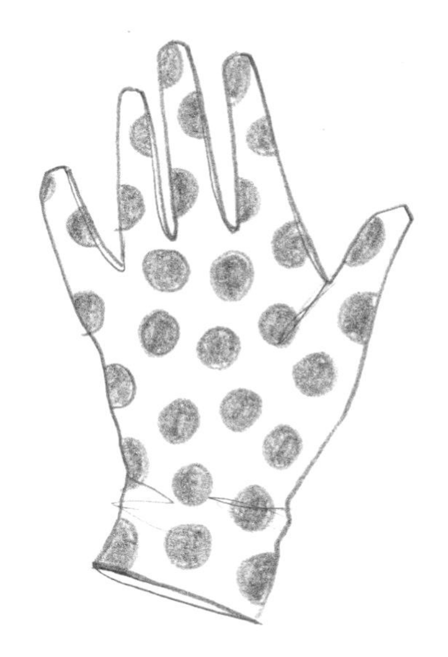
Gloves with prints

Lace gloves

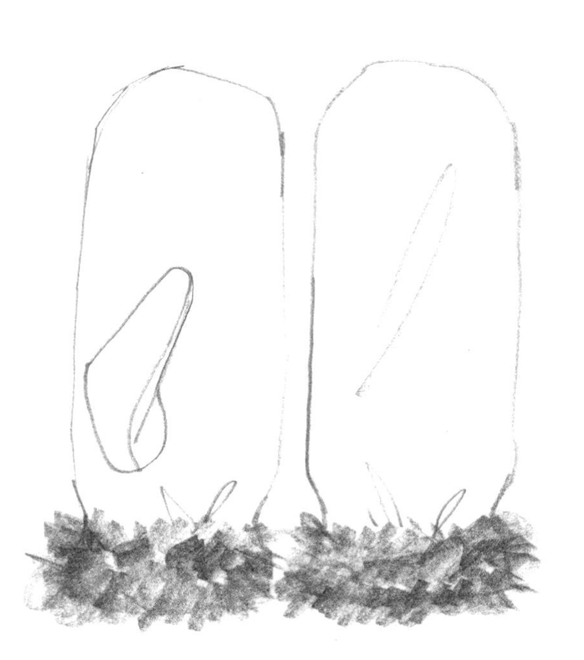
Mittens

Sunglasses

Broad-brimmed hat
with flower

Cowboy hat

Hat with scarf

Top hat

Scarves, *front* and *profile*

1970s cap

Boys cap

Earmuffs

Knitted hat

Beret

Headbands

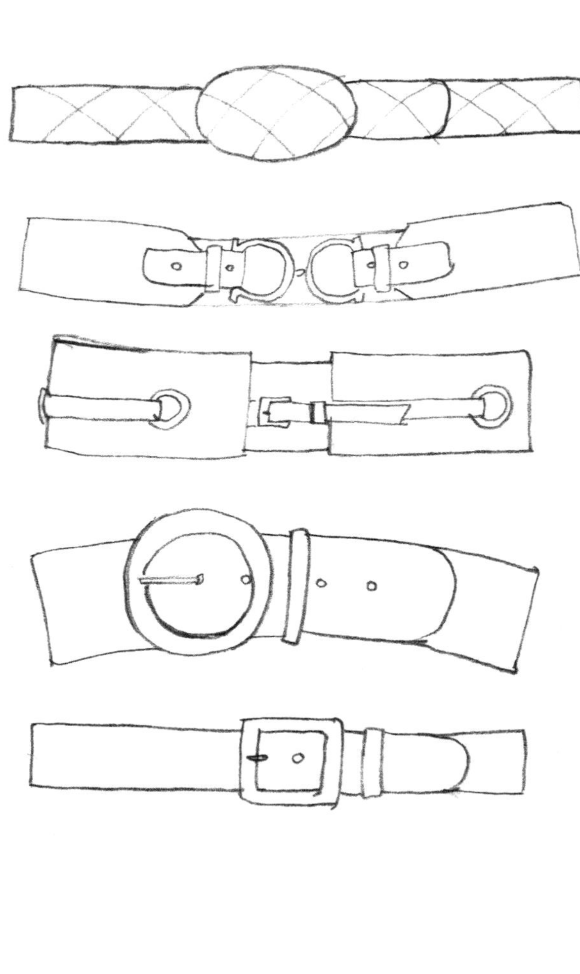

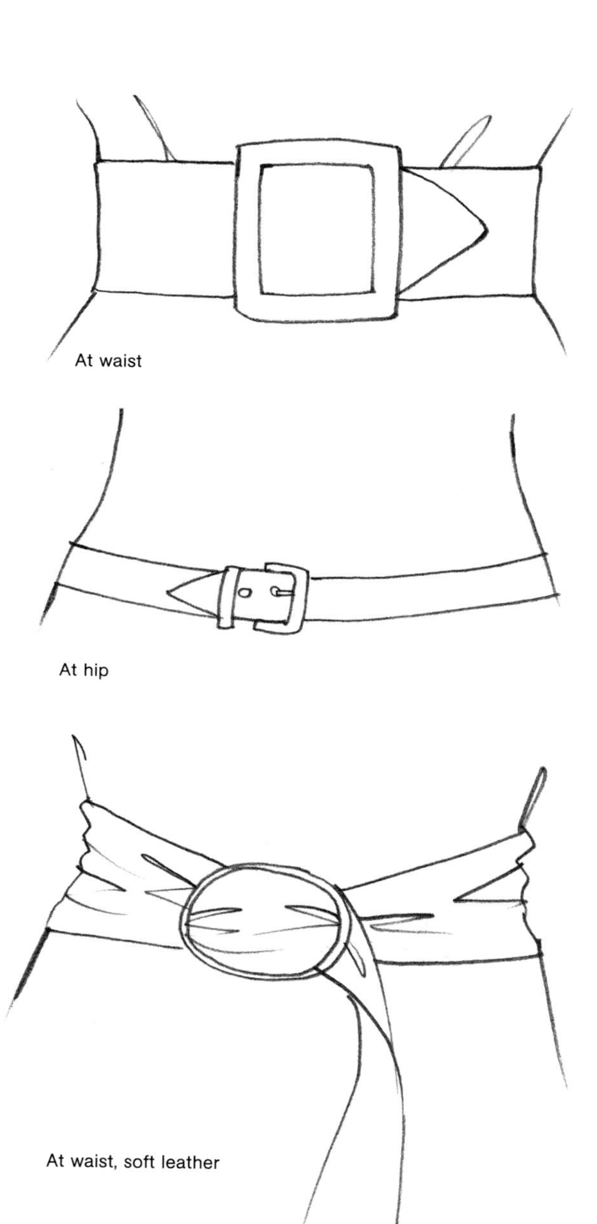

Belts

At waist, soft leather